Praise for Gary Quinn

"Gary is here to shake us up, wake us up and show us to ourselves."

Leeza Gibbons
TV entertainment personality/producer and
CEO of The Memory Center Foundation

"Gary's gentle, remarkable book is a must read for anyone on a spiritual path. Read and glow."

Denise Linn
author of *Soul Coaching: 28 Days to Discover Your Authentic Self*

"Gary Quinn is pure inspiration! Enjoy your journey into the Spiritual Zone—you couldn't have a better guide and teacher!"

Stephanie Saible
editor-in-chief, *Woman's World*

"This amazing book gives you the tools you need to be in your power"

Esther Williams
MGM's aquatic sensation, *New York Times* best-selling author, *The Million Dollar Mermaid*

"Let Gary Quinn take you on the journey of your life and you just might not want to come back! Release your innermost fears and open yourself up to your potential."

Dr. Eric Pearl
healer and international best-selling author of
The Reconnection: Heal Others, Heal Yourself

"Gary Quinn is supremely insightful and equipped with the knowledge to alter perceptions. With his guidance, life's challenges can become positive, fulfilling experiences. His wisdom is utterly modern."

Vogue

"Gary Quinn is the missing link, the new spiritual messenger."

InStyle **magazine**

W9-CPC-188

"*Living in the Spiritual Zone* is a rare mix of simple truths, helping us give up our dramas and get out of our own way. This book is a banquet for the soul."

James Twyman
film producer of *Indigo,* and best-selling author of *Emissary of Light*

"Gary's gentle words ignite the desire to comprehend and the self-motivation to attain the Universal energies we all hold as a key to manifesting our potential."

Brit Elders
CEO—*ShirleyMacLaine.com*

"Gary Quinn offers truth, love and spiritual wisdom in a highly readable book. With clarity and divinely guided intention, he shines a very bright light on the path of love."

Arielle Ford
author of *Magical Souvenirs: True Spiritual Adventures from Around the World*

"Gary opens us up to endless possibilities . . . and tells us that all we have to do is . . . reach for them."

Sharon Tay
MSNBC-TV host, *MSNBC at the Movies*

LIVING IN THE SPIRITUAL ZONE

Also by Gary Quinn

May the Angels Be with You

Living in the Spiritual Zone—Messages and Meditations
(4 CD-AUDIO PROGRAM)

Nine Keys to Awaking Your Spirit by Using the Power Within
(AUDIO)

LIVING IN THE SPIRITUAL ZONE

10 Steps to Change
Your Life and Discover Your Truth

GARY QUINN

Health Communications, Inc.
Deerfield Beach, Florida

www.hcibooks.com

Library of Congress Cataloging-in-Publication Data

Quinn, Gary.
　　Living in the spiritual zone : 10 steps to change your life and discover your truth /
Gary Quinn.
　　　　p. cm.
　　Includes bibliographical references.
　　ISBN-13: 978-0-7573-0324-1
　　ISBN-10: 0-7573-0324-2
　　　　1. Spiritual life.　2. Self-actualization (Psychology)—Religious aspects.　I. Title.

BL624.Q53　2005
204'.4—dc22

2005046230

Publisher:　Health Communications, Inc.
　　　　　　3201 S.W. 15th Street
　　　　　　Deerfield Beach, FL 33442-8190

R-08-07

Cover design by Kevin Stawieray
Inside book design by Dawn Von Strolley Grove

I dedicate this book to spiritual seekers worldwide.

Those who follow and trust their inner path

will experience only greatness in life.

Contents

Introduction

Congratulations! By acquiring this book, you have made the choice to journey to the Spiritual Zone, a welcoming place of trust, peace, love, belonging, joy and abundance. If you have felt frustrated, stuck, lonely, worried, needy or broke it, may very well be due to limited assumptions you have held (consciously or unconsciously) of what is possible for your life. The Spiritual Zone is a panorama of unlimited possibility, a place within yourself where you can access and fully enjoy all the resources of the Universe as your lawful birthright as an integral part of the great All That Is. The Spiritual Zone is only a step away from where you are living your limited life right now; to get you to the Zone I will help you to reconnect to your true identity, which is love. We will use truth and forgiveness as our primary tools.

At our core, we are all spiritual beings, yet the gravity of our physical environment and the fierce cultural pull of materialism has caused many of us to forget this essential truth about ourselves. My intention with this book is to reawaken you to the memory that you are indeed a spiritual being and that the natural expression of your spirituality is love. Consider me your travel guide on the adventure of your new life.

Imagine a few moments in your life when something astonishingly beautiful startled you momentarily out of your ordinary routine—a stunning, rosy sunrise rolling towards you, the wide arc of a double rainbow, deep eye contact with a baby, the surprise appearance of a hummingbird, an unexpected kindness from a stranger. Any number of incidents can suddenly awaken us more fully to the beauty and goodness of life; these surprise moments of heightened consciousness are peeks into the wonder of the Spiritual Zone, where all of life is essentially good and beautiful.

Whether you realize it or not, your life on earth is directed by the choices you create for yourself—consciously or unconsciously—in the Spiritual Zone. It is in the Spiritual Zone that you write the script that you in turn act out on the stage of physical reality. We are—each and every one of us—high spiritual beings in various degrees of development. With the conscious acceptance of this truth, we flow into love, peace and abundance, but we ebb away when fear and illusion pull us into a contracted, self-protective state. When we are aligned with our spiritual selves we find guidance, peace, prosperity, partnership, connection, compassion, love, purpose and all levels of fulfillment. Yet, we are frequently distracted from our spiritual truth by limiting fears, self-doubts, judgment and all the lures of materialism. Through the guidance and examples in this book, I hope to inspire you to choose truth, no matter what, and to use an ongoing practice of forgiveness to identify and heal the illusions that separate you from the majestic love and light that are your birthright as a spiritual being. Think of this journey as a homecoming. Welcome back to where you belong.

I first entered consciously into the Spiritual Zone many years ago in the Cathedral of Notre-Dame in Paris. I had moved to Paris after having been offered a recording contract. I had quit my job and given up my life in Los Angeles only to arrive in Paris and learn that the contract had been canceled. The disappointment was so great that I went into a complete emotional tailspin. Desperate for guidance, I went to Notre-Dame every day for three weeks and prayed for a sign telling me what I should do. On the third day of the third week, I experienced a life-changing vision. I was sitting alone in the quiet of the near-empty cathedral when I was suddenly beckoned to look up. From the ceiling, a purple light flowed down on to me, and then I could see angels dancing around me. They spoke to me telepathically, telling me to trust that I was meant to be in Paris and that I would be guided and cared for. They awakened me to the spiritual aspects of myself that create and energize my physical being. They instantaneously communicated to me an experience of the profound spiritual world at work behind common physical reality—and that it is in this spiritual place where the work of creating our lives truly happens. I learned quickly that I could access this place through a practice of love, truth and forgiveness, and I learned that my mission is to teach others about this deeper aspect of their beings. I've come to think of this inner place as the Spiritual Zone.

The Spiritual Zone is a state of being, complete with its own entry protocols, language, customs, codes of conduct, diet, manners, responsibilities and ethics. Some of you may feel a bit uncertain traveling into what feels like such unfamiliar territory; others will be more ready to feel at home from the beginning, recognizing parts of the Zone culture from previous spiritual journeys; still others among you will immediately recognize this trip to the Spiritual Zone as the blessed homecoming that it truly is. In any case, I am here to guide you. I will be the one to remind you of local customs, direct you in your possible confusion, and reassure you if from time to time you doubt that you have hooked up with the right tour.

In seeking your own Spiritual Zone, some of you are traveling from greater distances than others, the circumstances of your previous life experiences perhaps having lured you far, far away from your spiritual home. It doesn't matter because we can travel faster than the speed of light: we travel at the speed of insight. I will offer you roadmaps, pictures and perspectives; I will present tools and guidance and support; I will coach you into confidence and excellence until you feel perfectly at home back where you first came from and where you always belong—the Spiritual Zone.

I am here to remind you that we are all spiritual beings. We choose to incarnate into bodies for the wealth of experiences that physical reality offers us. Our bodies allow us to see, hear, touch, taste and smell; they allow us magnificent and unique contact with other incarnated spiritual beings. Our bodies enable us in so many ways, yet they are not us; they are only tools of our yearning to experience. If we choose to see our bodies as tools, we will have taken the first step beyond them and into identifying with the far grander spiritual beings who are our true unlimited selves, our royal selves.

In the Spiritual Zone we recognize that we are not now—and never have been—limited by the constraints we mistakenly assign to our physical selves and to physical reality. We awaken to the possibility of ourselves as truly creative beings who have fashioned these physical existences for ourselves. As such, we remember that we chose to incarnate into physicality for all the countless opportunities of this experience.

In the Zone our perspective shifts from feeling constrained by life's limits to appreciating the unlimited creative potential that our royal selves have embraced by returning to this realm.

This new perspective has countless practical applications. Once you access the Zone, you will recognize that this lifetime of ours is made up of infinite choices. You may awaken to the realization that you may have made an unconscious choice to be lonely, hungry, impoverished or unhappy. Now you can make a different choice! This is the speed of insight. Once you realize that you have set up your life's circumstances to teach yourself particular lessons, you can identify the lesson, integrate it into the vastness of your being, and choose to move on to something less painful and more uplifting.

You *can* get there from here. You are already on your way. I am your guide. Through my conscious intention, I *live* in the Spiritual Zone, and you do too, even if you have forgotten. I am your traveling companion through the process of remembering. By acquiring this guidebook, you have already taken the first step toward the Spiritual Zone: you have made the choice to invite change into your life. This seemingly simple act has alerted your guides, angels and spiritual allies to be on standby to assist you in your great awakening.

The journey to the Spiritual Zone can be addressed much like any other trip. If you were planning to travel to Italy for a summer vacation, wouldn't you prepare for your trip by learning what you could about the local people and their customs? How do Italians behave toward one another? How do they act? What are their social protocols? What could you learn about their language? What is the local diet? Do they exercise?

Even the excited anticipation of an Italian vacation might be tinged with a little anxiety: you are, after all, leaving the comfort of familiarity (no matter how uncomfortable) for an unknown place. No matter that you will experience the grandness of Michelangelo's *David* and the hand of God on the ceiling of the Sistine Chapel, the romance of seeing Venice by gondola and the thrill of tooling high along the Amalfi coast in your Alfa Romeo with Mediterranean breezes rushing through your hair—until you arrive and are captivated by these wonderful experiences, *until they become known to you,* they will likely be accompanied by some anxiety of the unknown. How do you flag a gondola? Where do you rent an Alfa Romeo? How do you order pasta? How do you bring knowledge to the unknown? I am here to be your guide, happy to direct you to fulfillment of all your desires in the Spiritual Zone.

So let me tell you a little about our trip. I've divided our itinerary into three parts:

1. How to Get to the Spiritual Zone
2. How to Stay in the Spiritual Zone
3. How to Manifest in the Spiritual Zone

First, we will consider the preparation for the journey: what to bring along, what to leave behind. This will require an honest examination of your current belief systems, because what you believe has created your life as you now know it. We'll consider the thought forms and emotional glues that keep us stuck to our realities, and we'll explore ways to free ourselves. Once we're ready for the journey, we'll travel to the Zone. How do we get there? Imagination, insight, practice—and a lot of letting go.

Consider yourself in training. I'll give you meditations and exercises to strengthen your body and your will for your trip. We'll learn about local customs and protocols—and diets: you'll learn how to nurture yourself in the spiritual latitudes.

In my work as a spiritual teacher, life coach-intuitive and writer, I travel a great deal, leading workshops and seminars and doing book tours. Not long ago, as I prepared a thirty-city lecture tour that would take me first to England and then throughout the United States, I heard my strong inner voice telling me there was something I needed to do to deepen the quality of my work. I had recently gone to an evening talk in Los Angeles given by a man named Serrano Kelly. This man said something that has changed me forever. He said, "You must have no regrets when you leave this earth."

This simple sentence struck me like a lightning bolt. I was deeply aware that I was getting this particular message at this particular time for a very particular purpose. I suddenly awakened to the realization that— even though I was intentionally living in the Spiritual Zone—I held regrets to redress, some emotional and spiritual housecleaning to take care of before I could authentically go on tour in the service of spiritual truth. I needed to deepen my access to the Zone.

I started looking at my relationships. I immediately felt three individuals with whom I was out of balance, with whom I was still out of truth. I had no time to procrastinate—I was leaving town! I called one of them, a former love with whom I had broken up during the writing of my first book, *May the Angels Be with You.* I'd been so busy with the book and with my other work that I hadn't been attentive to our relationship. I'd even missed our anniversary! This left my ex angry and frustrated. What could I do to heal this resentment? What could I do to make this right? I sent a huge bouquet of flowers with the note, "Happy Belated Anniversary!" and I made a dinner date, where I apologized for not being present to the relationship. Saying this opened the door for me to realize I'd always been somewhat blocked emotionally in that relationship. I hadn't shared myself at a deep spiritual level. I may have given a lot, but I hadn't given me. Looking at this truth about myself and how I had lived my life was so intense that I started crying right there in the restaurant. It was like a dam had burst, dissolving the blockages that had shaped my love life. My ex and I talked at length about each of our shortcomings and how they had caused resentments and regrets. We forgave each other and at once felt tremendously lighter. I forgave myself for the shortcomings of my past. Aligned now in the truth, we were freed of resentment and could go forward together as supportive friends.

I came home that night and called an artist friend named Harold Dupré, who lives in France. We have been close friends for fifteen years, but in all that time I have never acknowledged his gifts as an artist. And he's a wonderful, extremely talented artist! Until the moment when I contemplated my regrets from the perspective of the Spiritual Zone, I hadn't been able to see that I had—because of my own insecurities—withheld my acknowledgement from Harold. That night on the phone, I told him truthfully what a wonderfully talented artist he is; I poured on all the much-deserved praise I'd withheld for the previous years of our friendship. And I felt a soaring in my own heart, a remarkable, healing expansion. The more I gave to him, the more I felt I had to give. The more I could give to myself.

I was on a roll. The following morning I went to visit my mother. During the time I was growing up, my mother had several husbands. With all these stepfathers, we moved a lot; I went to sixteen schools in twelve years. In spite of all the stepfathers and the instability, I realize now that my mother did the very best she could as a mother. I sat next to her on her sofa and for the first time told her this, told her very directly she'd done a great job as my mom. I told her that I was deeply grateful for her love and knowledge and input and that I thought she was terrific. Her energy immediately changed. A tremendous, unacknowledged tension evaporated. I felt a huge, immediate shift—like a heavy facade of bricks was falling off me. My mom hugged me and I suddenly knew that we could now have a contemporary, honest relationship.

This was the Spiritual Zone working in me. Before I could journey to England to share the spiritual insights related to my *Angels* book, my spiritual self required me to let go of the toxic resentments and regrets that my less conscious self had held on to. I had no choice; I had to be clear in my own truth before I could begin to do the spiritual work that was calling me. Before I could talk, I had to walk my talk. In the course of these candid conversations I felt myself expand from Gary the lecturer and intuitive to Gary the sharer of truth. And in that truth I have become miraculously closer to each of these individuals than I had ever been before. In my intention to live in the Spiritual Zone, I've become Gary in the flow and service of spirituality.

In each of these relationships, I had withheld something: acknowledgement, approval, praise, love, my true feelings, and my self. It was fear that had caused me to hold back, fear that if I gave these folks the love or recognition that they deserved, there would be something less for myself. Instead of being a fountain of abundant spiritual truth, I'd been functioning as a valve, acting as if there were limited goodness to go around, as if by acknowledging the goodness in others there would be less goodness left over for me. In the Spiritual Zone, I know that the opposite is true. The more we allow our spiritual truth to flow freely through us, the more we make ourselves available to the surprising and miraculous gifts that our spirituality provides.

When we are coming from truth, from higher consciousness, our desires change, and we have a completely different relationship to them. In the Spiritual Zone we trust that our desires are healthy and honorable. There is no delusional competition telling me that my desires can only be met at the exclusion of someone else's. We do not have to settle for compromised situations that reflect our unworthiness. I can seek to fulfill my true desires directly, with love and without guilt that my gain will cause anyone else loss. By embracing opportunities to fulfill my true self, I am honoring the One True Self, the All That Is, of which I am an integral part. In the Spiritual Zone, aligned with this whole, I know that my true desires are achieved without cost to anyone else—because in truth there is no scarcity or lack. My gain is your gain. Your gain is my gain, for in truth we are all one. In this truth I bring a whole different self to all my situations and relationships and undertakings. I am no longer defending my separateness; instead, I act in all decisions toward union and reunion. The result is a deeply satisfying experience of spiritual *flow*. This is the nature of life in the Zone.

In order to give yourself a picture of what life is like in the Spiritual Zone, take a moment and think of yourself as a fountain. Maybe you're the famed Trevi Fountain in Rome, or a familiar fountain in your own neighborhood. Universal energy flows through you, bubbling up from its infinite depths and surging outwards. Your magnificent flow sustains you and all that comes in contact with you; it is refreshing, inspiring, invigorating. You project affirmation, abundance, affluence and love. The Universal source flows an unlimited supply of energy, love, power, ideas—of all sustenance—through you and majestically out into the world.

You are a fountain in the service of your spirituality. This picture of yourself is a passport. Tune in for a moment and feel the rush of your spiritual energy stream through you. This is your divine right. You are a channel of the source. You are showering Universal energy upon yourself, your family and friends, upon all whom you come in contact with—causing smiles to awaken, ideas to spring forth, hearts and flowers to blossom.

Stop now, and think of yourself as a valve.

You have taken it upon yourself to regulate the flow of Universal energy, rationing the amount of goodness, love and prosperity in your life—for fear these gifts of spirit will become depleted and run out. As a valve, you work in the service of scarcity, doubt and fear, the great limiters. Your mind operates under the illusion that there is not enough. You spend your life worrying about lack. You feel yourself grow rigid, contracted, brittle, stuck. Your mind is rationing life—and with it love, prosperity and happiness.

How do you want to live your life: as a fountain or as a valve? Furthering the flow, or limiting the flow? In the abundant Zone or in the delusion of scarcity? If you have identified with the valve instead of the *source* of the flow, you have usurped the authority of the Universe. You are living in opposition to spirit. No wonder you can't seem to have what you want in life—*you have been opposing the source.*

If you are not flowing in life, you are not really living. Nothing comes to you as a final destination in life; it only flows through you. Your rational—rationing—mind will never accept this, but you are the giver of the source, and the source offers unlimited energy, ideas, love, trust and power that enrich your life and fulfill your every desire as they flow through you and out into the world.

If this book has found its way into your hands, then you are being called home by your spirituality. Throughout this book, we will work together to restore you to your royal birthright: the Spiritual Zone. Together we will engage your ever-expanding heart in a practice of love, forgiveness and truth. We will see to it that you begin to flow.

In the beginning of this journey, you must be ready to stand in the total acceptance of fear, of attachment, of giving and of receiving. Anything about yourself that you have held in darkness must be brought into the light. *Only through the forgiving acceptance of the whole truth of yourself can you be truly available to love in all its miraculous manifestations.* Love is our essence as spiritual beings; it meets all our needs and heals all our disease. Accepting your complete truth right now is the portal through the petty worries of your rational mind and into the loving grandeur of the Spiritual Zone.

Your ego-mind controls with doubt and fear, playing tricks on everything you do in life—*but only if you let it.* You must be willing to have your fear, so that it doesn't have you. Contained in the heart, the bodily center of spiritual energy, your fears will evaporate.

Your divine right is now. Each experience in your life is an opportunity to move deeper into your spiritual quest. Through the course of this book, as you practice forgiveness and trust, you will begin to stand in truth. The limiting illusions of your rational mind will fall away as it gives over your identity to your infinite, loving spiritual self. In the Zone you will find yourself living in the wondrous flow of love, and you, too, will soar.

The way my spiritual self directed me to bring my past relationships into right alignment before I could begin my lecture tour is one example of the specific guidance that comes to us when we awaken to our identities as spiritual beings. By finding yourself on this page in this book, you, too, are being called to bring your life into alignment with your spiritual purpose—*right now,* at this very moment. Come home to your real purpose: *love.* Love of yourself, love of others, love of all life. You can access your purpose through the twin practices of truth and forgiveness. This book is an immediate opportunity for you to learn, recognize and remember that you are a connected, loving, spiritual being. In the Spiritual Zone you will experience constant communion with the one source, and you will know you are entitled to all that you want in life. The source has directed me to reach out to you with these ideas and exercises, to find you and guide you home.

There will be challenges as we move forward through this book together. Attachments to materialism cling powerfully and old habits die hard. We've invested heavily in the delusions of physical reality. We've told ourselves that we don't deserve love, that for any number of reasons we aren't good enough. We think we have done things that are unforgivable. We have habitually judged others as better and worse than ourselves, in both cases with the result of setting ourselves apart from them. We have preferred to think of ourselves as isolated, solitary individuals, and we've concocted all kinds of reasons to convince ourselves that we are undeserving of deep contact with others and of communion with spirit.

These are the habits of the ego as it struggles for sovereignty over our lives; the ego that fears it will be crushed and abandoned if we enter the

Zone and surrender control of our lives to spirit. Letting go of a vigilant, determined-to-be-sovereign ego can be difficult; this is our ongoing challenge as we confront the choice of love versus fear.

The ambivalence you may feel at the outset of this journey and the struggle you may experience as you travel through this book are the reactions of your fear-based, self-protective ego not wanting to surrender to your higher consciousness. Until now, this ego has functioned as an effective gatekeeper, keeping you safe from its perceived dangers—and for this it must be honored. It has also deprived you of the grandeur of your spirituality by subscribing to the illusion that you are only your bodily self—for this it must be forgiven.

As we move forward together towards the higher consciousness of the Spiritual Zone, you will outgrow the tight confines of the ego. Through the message and exercises of this book, you will come to identify with your infinitely expansive spiritual self—which will neither crush nor abandon the ego, but rather lovingly contain it, appreciate it for its appropriate usefulness and forgive its delusions of sovereignty. By acquiring this book, by your very curiosity about journeying to the Spiritual Zone, you are embarking on a noble and holy quest for love. Truth and forgiveness are your invincible tools. A full heart, abundance and a deeply felt communion with all of life will be your just rewards.

Shall we go?

Part One

How to Get to the Spiritual Zone

1
Waking Up Your Awareness

Just as you would have started planning your fantasy Italian vacation months in advance, so too have you been planning for this adventure into the Spiritual Zone—for your whole life. Everything you have been and done has brought you exactly to this point. Every thought, feeling and experience you have had has contributed to the whole of you that you are right now—appreciate them all with gratitude that they have brought you to a tremendous spiritual opportunity on this very page at this very moment. Regrets? Sure, you've had a few—you might have awoken and got here a few months or years or even decades earlier—but remember, please, that all mistakes are learning opportunities: once bitten, twice shy. So even your mistakes have directed you to this very moment—refining your path to your point of departure.

Consider that when you were born you were in a pretty sleepy state; in fact, you spent much more than half of each day sleeping. As you have matured you have grown more and more awake; your body probably only sleeps now eight or fewer hours a day—only a third each day. You have matured from a child concerned only with survival to a self-conscious adult concerned now with how to awaken even more consciousness in yourself. Instead of questing for food and shelter and love and sex and comforts as you have done during previous developmental stages in your life, now you are setting out on your quest for spiritual meaning—and all the magic that comes with it.

You are not alone on this journey. In fact, you travel in royal company. Preceding you on the quest have been the great mystics and philosophers and initiates, for this quest had once been reserved for the spiritual elite. Times have changed. Consider the changes to physical life during the past 200 years. Even in the most prosperous countries, human beings were living very simple lives in 1800: plowing by mule, reading by candlelight, writing with quills and sending letters by horseback. Yet even these recent ancestors were well on their way to the sweeping materialism that has captivated Western and world society today. Forget plowing and planting: we now buy our factory-farmed food ripe, picked, washed, irradiated, seasoned, preserved, pre-cooked, packaged and ready for the microwave. We watch movies and listen to books on tape; we communicate by e-mail at the speed of light.

The pull of materialism brings with it inherent dissatisfactions: we have lost touch, literally, with the earth. Think about this: how often does your skin touch soil? Except for our humanized house pets, we have also lost contact with the animal kingdom. Your great-great-great-grandfather's partnership with his mule as they walked together through fields was one of the most important cooperative ventures of his life. The pause to dip his quill into his inkwell enforced frequent thoughtful moments. I imagine there was a built-in connectedness to other beings 200 years ago that sustained the spiritual lives of our great-grandparents' grandparents.

Today, we feign a connectedness to the whole of life, trying to pretend that our broadband hook-up to the World Wide Web is in itself meaningful. Yes, we can e-mail friends and strangers anywhere in the world within a matter of seconds. Sure, this is a fantastic tool—but how many times, honestly, has it enriched your spiritual life?

I believe that the descent into materialism brings with it its balancing opposite: the quest for spiritual experience. This is the very quest that drives you and me to be here together now. No doubt this hunger for spiritual experience is widely present and growing. Look at book sales statistics: self-help books are the biggest growing sector of publishing. Look how the aerobics and workout craze of the eighties has been eclipsed now by yoga studios on every block; this is a perfect demonstration of how in a very short period we have grown from being (somewhat self-indulgently) focused on our physical selves to now demanding that our workout time feeds our spiritual as well as our bodily needs.

This is all to say that you are not alone on this journey to the Spiritual Zone. Human beings are traveling to the Zone in far greater numbers than ever before. Just as you can travel to Italy by air, land or sea, people access the Zone through a multitude of means—including study of books like this, lectures, meditation, numerous spiritual practices, yoga and prayer.

All of these include the requirement of self-study. Getting to know who you are better and why you are who you are will accelerate your readiness for our departure. This will be the focus of this chapter as we wake up our consciousness in light of our three primary human components: our bodies, our minds and our hearts.

Preparing Your Body for the Spiritual Zone

Our bodies are the temples of our spirits. If we don't feed the right things to our bodies, we won't be in alignment to stay tuned and receive the messages and guidance we need. We also won't have the energy and stamina to do the work we are here to do.

I know good health—diet and exercise—is critically important for me to keep clearly tuned in to my feelings and my guidance. As we have begun to awaken as a people, we have become more aware of the importance of healthy diet. We are told we will live longer and better lives. You know what? We will also live truer lives. We must feed our bodies appropriately so that they may serve our spiritual selves effectively.

What (and how much) we take into our bodies has a profound effect on our vibrations—the rate at which our nervous systems and cellular structure harmonize with the frequencies of the Universe. If we are dulled by alcohol or overeating, our sluggish vibration can contain only heavy energy. If we are wired on caffeine or sugar, our frenetic vibration channels only scattered energy. If we are poisoned by animal antibiotics and excess hormones, our bodies will be incapable of settling into the harmonious silence where our guidance is waiting. Remember my experience in Notre-Dame in Paris? I had been meditating quietly for three weeks.

Our appetites and cravings are established by our past mistakes (which set up metabolic, as well as psychological, expectations) and by tremendous commercial and cultural influences. Simple, detoxifying diets can purify us of these influences and expectations, clearing the opportunity for truth to let us know what our bodies need in order to house and accommodate our spiritual missions more effectively.

Rather than making us slimmer, sexier, more beautiful, popular or successful—as our media-driven consumer culture would have us believe—the real need for a healthy diet is to become awake and truly available to our spiritual purpose. Once we have taken a decisive step in this direction, our bodies will act in joyful service of our spiritual intentions—and we'll find old cravings and attractions will have lost their powerful appeal. There is an old saying: "You are what you eat." Well, truly, you are what you think, but how you think is greatly affected by what you eat. So let's start with diet.

Eating for True Health in the Spiritual Zone

The word "diet" is loaded with associations of overweight people wanting to slim down, hoping that depriving themselves of some kind of food indulgence will make them trimmer, happier and more loveable. Diet books, too, are constantly making their way onto the bestseller lists. Yet obesity continues to plague the Western world. Why is this? What are people so hungry for that they continually and obsessively overeat?

I believe that the vast majority of overweight people are feeding themselves to numb the pain of their alienated lives. Our consumer culture has led not-so-awake people to think that the more and better material things they possess, the more fulfilled they will feel. Yet this is not the case. Many people eat to fill the spiritual void in their lives. Some of you who are reading this book with me now are overweight. Some of you have been eating to comfort the anxiety and alienation that are inherent in a culture that has made consumerism its idol. To you, my friends, I say welcome home.

In the Spiritual Zone you will experience a connectedness with and a belonging to the unity of all of life. Your loneliness will evaporate as you learn to forgive your mistaken (and unconscious) beliefs about separation. Food will become true pleasure and sustenance instead of compulsion. In the Spiritual Zone you will recognize your deepest hunger as spiritual longing, and you will know that this longing is already satisfied.

If you were planning to spend your summer exploring the hill towns of Italy, you'd want to make certain that your body was prepared for the local challenges—the steep cobblestone streets, the world's best pasta and gelato on every street corner. You might do very well to eat healthfully for the few months prior to your departure, knowing that you are more likely to enjoy the trip if your body can keep up with your interests. Preparing for your Italian vacation is an opportunity to bring more consciousness to your diet. Italy pervades your thoughts; it's easier to pass up that second serving of chocolate decadence because you know by doing so you'll feel and look better by the pool. Planning for your trip has made you more awake to your actions. It has brought more consciousness into your day-to-day decisions. The anticipation of your trip is already impacting your life.

So what should you eat/not eat in preparation for the Spiritual Zone? There is going to be a different answer for each of you. Our bodily needs are different, but what we can each immediately do in preparation for the journey is to wake up to our eating practices. Make eating a conscious practice. This way, you will be more likely to eat only what you truly want. This heightened awareness can be applied to whole meals, snacks and even individual bites. By consciously choosing each bite that you take, you are welcoming that particular food into your body. It then becomes your sustenance, serving your health and all your capacities. As you enter into the Spiritual Zone, you will learn that, in awakened consciousness, every action, no matter how small, will intentionally support your end result.

There was a period when I was considerably overweight. I was numb and unhappy and half-asleep. Eating was my solace, but I did not particularly enjoy food. I barely even tasted it. I enjoyed the pleasure of the anticipation of each bite of cookies 'n' cream, but, to be honest, the moment each bite touched my tongue it mingled with regret. I didn't truly enjoy it; I didn't savor it. I swallowed it—gulped it, really—so I could get back to the pleasure of anticipating the next bite. Each of those ambivalent bites of high butterfat ice cream was swallowed with disdain and regret, more deeply damaging than even the richest hot fudge. I have since forgiven myself for this confused habit—it did serve to get me to where I am today, and for that I am grateful.

I share this personal example with you now to help wake you up to your own unconscious eating habits. Do you love your food; welcome it into your body as a source of nourishment and strength? Or do you resent it as you consume it, swallowing each bite with a big seasoning of negativity?

Now is the time to wake up to your eating practices. How? Here are some simple suggestions that will help you to bring consciousness to your meals:

1. **Shop consciously.** Choose healthful foods that will nourish and sustain your body. Buy fresh produce. Avoid ingesting chemical fertilizers and pesticides by purchasing organically grown products, which are also generally grown more consciously. Consider a vegetarian diet; most animals, in addition to being potentially diseased, are raised on antibiotics and artificial growth hormones, which are passed on to unwitting human consumers of meat. As well, I believe meat products are filled with animal adrenaline, produced by the animal's profound fear at the point of its killing. Mad cow disease was a gift to the spiritualization of the English diet. Do be aware though, that not everyone can tolerate a vegetarian diet as some people cannot digest pulses or soy. The key thing, if you do eat animal proteins, is to choose organic, as far as possible. Avoid the regular use of sugar and caffeine: these hollow energy sources take your body on a roller-coaster ride of artificially induced highs and crashing lows. Experiment with a reduced wheat or wheat-free diet in order to feel lighter and more energized.

2. **Get to know your farmer.** Today, many communities have farmers' markets and many in my country have community supported agriculture (CSA) programs where people come together and support local organic farmers by purchasing a share of the farmer's crop in advance and receiving a weekly box of fresh produce in

return. A personal relationship with your farmer gives each bite you take more context. Even better—grow your own!

3. **Prepare your own meals.** Allow cooking to become a ritual of nourishment. Imbue your food with your intentional consciousness by washing it, cutting it and preparing it carefully and beautifully with mindfulness. I believe lovingly and intentionally prepared food contains some of the life-force (chi) of its preparer; this is the profound gift of a fully conscious chef. Factory-made foods and fast foods are prepared by machines and doused with preservatives; be aware that the primary intent in their production is profit for the manufacturers' stockholders, not loving nourishment for you.

4. **Set your table beautifully.** The ritual of setting flowers, candles, attractive dishes and cutlery and cloth napkins will awaken the intentional consciousness that turns eating into dining.

5. **Only eat sitting down—and never in your car!** This will force you to be present with the meal in front of you. When eating (literally) on the run, driving or standing up, you are not giving your meal the time or attention it deserves; your consciousness is already on to your next activity. Your body deserves your full attention during eating; if you pay attention, you will be more awake to what you like, to when you are satisfied and how well you are being nourished.

6. **Say a blessing.** A moment of recognition that your meal is a gift from the source of all of life reestablishes your conscious connection to all living things.

7. **Eat with others.** Dining is a wonderful opportunity for communion. When we break bread with others we share ourselves as well as our food. This helps to heal the alienation that is so commonly experienced in modern culture.

8. **Be mindful of each bite.** Consciously choose each individual bite as you select it from your plate. Eat it because you have decided you truly want it, not simply because it is in front of you. In this way you are imbuing each bite you consume with your awakened consciousness so that it can better nurture your bodily needs.

9. **Enjoy the taste!** Swallow with conscious appreciation (not ambivalence or regret). You deserve the pleasurable tastes of your food.

10. **Recognize when you are satisfied.** All the above steps will help to awaken you to your eating process. You will soon be eating for eating's sake—pleasurably to nourish and sustain your physical body—instead of eating to numb pain or fill the void of alienation and loneliness. You will become increasingly able to detect your body's awareness that you have had enough, and then you will be happy to stop, feeling fully satisfied. You will learn the difference between feeling satisfied and feeling full.

11. **Be thankful.**

Exercising for Strength and Stamina in the Spiritual Zone

In addition to a well-nourished body, you will want a strong body for your journey into the Spiritual Zone. Just as you wouldn't want to miss out on visiting Assisi because your body was too out-of-shape to manage the steep climb, you won't want to miss all the magnificent opportunities of the Spiritual Zone—clear intuition, angelic guidance, deep spiritual contact with others.

You will want to wake up your body with conscious movement and exercise. By choosing to approach the Spiritual Zone, you have already made a choice to forgo numbing and awaken to your body. Now, by being present to your body, you can coach it to strength and stamina and flexibility. Don't worry that you have to become an Olympic athlete or an impressively posed yogi; simply get outside and walk around the block. Conscious movement encourages flexibility and fluidity; it dissolves blockages and enables the flow of energy.

In the Spiritual Zone you will be channeling more spiritual energy. As we discussed in the introduction, you will become a fountain of Universal spiritual energy. How big a fountain you become, how much spiritual energy you are able to conduct, depends upon your intent and your capacity. Your capacity is determined in large part by the health of your body. If you eat in alignment with the suggestions of this chapter, you will already bring more consciousness—more spiritual flow—into your body.

GET MOVING

Take ten minutes right now to walk around the block. I mean it. Finish this paragraph, and then put on your shoes and go. Walk briskly but comfortably. Feel into your body as if this were an altogether new and foreign experience. What is this body you have landed in? What are its capacities? Can it move quickly? Does it heat up when you go more quickly? Do you break a sweat? Can you find a comfortable rhythm as you gently swing your arms back and forth? What length of stride feels more comfortable and efficient? Does this help to propel you forward? What kind of breathing facilitates your walking? Does deep breathing give you more fuel? Do you land on your heels and push off with the balls of your feet? Are your hips moving? Are your shoulders? Is your head? Where do your eyes focus? Okay, now go. Enjoy your walk, and pay attention to yourself as you move through space.

Find time every day to do some physical exercise. As you have just discovered, a walk is good; walk briskly. Bike ride, swim, jog, dance, jump—move! Whatever you choose, pay attention to your body as you do it. Put your intention into the time spent. You're not simply walking around the block to get back to where you started; you're walking in order to wake up your body, your muscles and your nervous system, to encourage the flow of energy. Don't overexert yourself; don't beat yourself up. The intention is to awaken your body through conscious movement, to clear out your energy by opening to the flow of new energy throughout your body.

As you continue to develop the consciousness within the cells of your body through elementary exercise, you may come to a place where you feel drawn to explore exercise techniques with an overt spiritual intention, specifically yoga. First wake up your body, then listen to what it needs; you can trust that you will be directed to the right exercise program that continues to energize your body and your spirituality.

PREPARING YOUR MIND FOR THE SPIRITUAL ZONE

Too often, we behave like scientists in making our life's decisions. We compile data, collect documentation, analyze past experience, and figure, figure, figure, trying to make things work. This is the mind, operating out of fear, trying to avoid the repetition of past failures. These decisions of the mind are inevitably made from a defensive, limiting perspective. What do they provide? Information overload, but never intelligence. Our little minds make us crazy by trying to figure it all out.

Learning how to be silent is the secret access to the Spiritual Zone. In the great silence we experience the higher power moving through us. There we find our spirituality waiting with guidance and answers. With every decision we make, we need to tune in and invoke the energy of our hearts to guide us.

Remember that this chapter is about focusing our intention on waking up our awareness. By bringing intention—let's call it "mindfulness"— to what and how we eat and when and how we move in our bodies, we are also serving to focus our minds. To get to and manifest successfully in the Spiritual Zone requires that we wake up our bodies and our minds—as well as our hearts and emotional selves.

Earlier in this chapter we addressed the importance of awakening our minds to our physical activities of eating and movement. In doing so, we have already established the importance of mindfulness. All creativity begins with thinking. Nothing has ever been intentionally created that wasn't first thought about: buildings, sculptures, governments, businesses, even vacations to Italy. Intentional, conscious thinking is the first step in creating anything—whether a work of art, a machine, an organization or the life and love that you want.

Thought is creative, whether it is intentional or not, whether it is positive or not. If you haven't yet brought mindfulness and intentionality to your thinking, then your unintentional (unconscious) thinking has been doing the creating while you've been asleep at the wheel. For convenience, let's call this unconscious thinking "thoughting."

Thoughting transports us away from the Spiritual Zone, lulling us to sleep. It is not an intentional, awakening process—rather, it is unconscious, passive, often habitual, and susceptible to outside influences. (Ever realize you had an advertising slogan running through your head?) Worry is an example of thoughting, and in today's world worry thrives in the absence of mindfulness. Worry is not a conscious act of creative thinking that intends to find solutions to a concern; rather it is a dead thought loop that can become the subliminal background music of an unconscious mind. *It is nonetheless creative—unconsciously manifesting negativity into our lives!*

Thoughting, and worry in particular, pulls us away from the Spiritual Zone and keeps us mired where we don't want to be in life. If you worry that you're going to catch a cold or that your boyfriend is going to leave you or that you're not going to have enough money at the end of the month, guess what: you are creating these negative results for yourself by feeding them with your attention.

Throughout this book we will address fear and help you to discover ways to free yourself from the influence of fear. For now, let's start with mindfulness.

Just as you have committed to eliminating toxins from your body through healthy diet and moderate exercise, you will also want to eliminate toxins from your mind by waking up your thinking. What are you thinking about as you read this sentence? What else are you thinking about besides this sentence? How many layers of thoughting are going on beneath your thinking? There are many meditative techniques to bring calm and focus to your mind. Many practices concern themselves with stilling the mind of the ongoing chatter that clutters our thinking; other practices focus the mind on a particular object or mantra or puzzle, such as the Zen koan. Gathering and focusing our conscious thinking in this way exercises the mind, strengthens it against the habit of thoughting, and prepares us for more effective thinking as the way to create the life experiences that we truly want for ourselves.

BREATHING AS A MEDITATION ON MINDFULNESS

As we introduced exercise with the basic act of walking around the block, let's focus on our breathing as an initial, simple meditative act that focuses our minds.

Find a comfortable sitting position, but not so comfortable that you are inclined to sleep. Remember, our intention here is to become *more* awake. You could sit on the floor in cross-legged lotus pose, or sit in a straight chair with both feet flat on the floor. Allow your shoulders to relax. Your hands lie relaxed on your thighs, palms up. Close your eyes. Now, give all your attention to your breath. Notice how you are breathing without yet manipulating your breathing. Are you breathing shallowly into only the upper portion of your lungs? This is a common habit.

Let's bring some deeper intentionality to our breathing. Sitting in your relaxed but not too comfortable position, picture your torso as a five-gallon jug that you might find on a water cooler. If you were to take this empty, upright jug and fill it with water, the water would first fill the bottom, and then rise gradually to the neck of the bottle. Imagine this bottle residing in your torso, from your navel (far deeper than the bottom of your lungs) to your throat. Consciously exhale all the stale air out of this bottle, slowly and deliberately—every last drop. Now, just as slowly and deliberately, fill the bottle back up, starting at the bottom and slowly rising to the top. Trust that your body is getting plenty of oxygen as you allow yourself about twenty seconds to fill up your torso. Once you reach capacity, begin to exhale slowly, first the air at the top of the bottle, then deeper, deeper, deeper, until you have expelled every last molecule of air from the bottom of your belly. Now, slowly and intentionally, begin filling the bottle back up again, breathing first into the bottom and then slowly filling all the way to the top. And continue.

I call this "bottle breathing." It is enormously effective in calming, yet energizing, your body. Bottle breathing oxygenates your cells far more successfully than typical shallow breathing. These are reasons in themselves for regularly practicing bottle breathing, but our primary intent in doing it now is to bring the mind under our control. Focusing our mental observation, our mindfulness, on our breathing brings an awakened intentionality to our thinking. This is a critical skill for a successful resident of the Spiritual Zone because wakefulness itself is the path to our deeper spiritual selves. It is through concentrated intention that we can create the lives that we truly want.

You may find during the practice of bottle breathing that your mind drifts from the intended focus on your breath. When you notice you have drifted, simply bring your mind back to your breath. If you are inclined to chastise yourself for failure, forgive yourself for drifting, then get back to the task at hand: intentional mindful breathing. Guilt is as worthless a distraction as the interrupting thought you might have decided to feel guilty about. Just continue to shepherd yourself back to the practice. This is a lifelong practice—forgive your transgressions and reapply yourself in service to your intention.

If particular thoughts—did you forget to return a friend's phone call? What's for dinner? That nagging pile of bills—persistently interrupt your focus on your breathing, restore your intention and from your conscious mindfulness look at those thoughts as apart from yourself; listen to them apart from yourself. You will find that, separated from your thinking, they have no life force. By considering your thoughting from a place of mindful thinking, the distracting thoughting withers and evaporates. Notice this, then return to your simple task of mindfully filling and emptying your torso of breath.

This practice for ten or fifteen minutes two or three times a day—or whenever you feel scattered or tired or anxious—will bring your mind back into focus and your thinking back into control of your thoughting. Each time you practice this, it strengthens your mental clarity—a key skill in helping you to access the Spiritual Zone.

There are countless other practices for awakening and exercising your mind. Consider:

OBJECT MEDITATION AS TRAINING FOR THINKING

Choose an ordinary object—a pencil or a paperclip. Decide that you will take ten minutes to focus your concentration on the contemplation of this object. Focus your mind first upon the immediate physical qualities of this object, your pencil. What is it made of? Graphite, wood, yellow paint, a brass fitting, a rubber eraser. Are there words printed on it? Are they embossed into the surface of the wood? How many sides does the pencil have? How long is it? How well used is the eraser? What shade is the yellow paint? How sharp is the point? Consider every physical aspect of the pencil as if you are touring its surface. You don't want to miss a single quality. When you have completed this, go deeper into the pencil. What kind of wood is it made of? Imagine the wood from this pencil being part of a larger block of wood. See that block of wood being cut from a still larger piece. See that piece being milled from a tree trunk. See the tree being transported to the mill. See the tree being felled. See the timber engineer choosing the tree. See the tree among other trees. See the forest among other terrains. See the seed cone from which the seed of this tree came. See its early beginning as a sprout. See the rains that nurtured it. See all the history and qualities that grew to become the wood of this pencil in your hand.

Now, likewise, consider the graphite, the paint, the brass that holds the eraser, the rubber eraser. Consider each element of the pencil, always mindful of what it has taken to become part of this pencil you hold in your hand. Maintain your mindfulness of the whole pencil as you contemplate its individual parts. This is your intention here: to sharpen and at the same time deepen your awareness of this rarely considered, relatively simple, ordinary object. Do this exercise daily for a week or longer, each day going deeper into your understanding of what this pencil is. After a time, choose another object and start over. The intent is to strengthen the focus of your mind and your thinking so that these capacities may be used effectively in service of your spiritual choices.

Mantra Meditation to Quiet the Mind

Long a part of yogic and Eastern spiritual practices, mantra meditation involves the focused repetition of a chosen word or phrase. The intention, again, is to focus the mind away from random thoughting. In some practices, such as Transcendental Meditation (TM), the practitioner is given a personal mantra by a spiritual teacher. In certain yogic practices there are countless different mantras that intend different specific results. If you are familiar with any of these practices, you will find all of them beneficial in training the mind away from random thoughting and into conscious thinking.

To practice mantra meditation, find a comfortable sitting position, either cross-legged on the floor, or on an upright chair, hands on your lap or thighs, eyes closed. Select a mantra that you are familiar with, make one up for yourself or try something like this:

"Love"
"I Am Love"
"God and Me, Me and God, Are One"

By experimenting with the practices suggested in this chapter you are readying your body and mind for your journey to the Spiritual Zone. Continued practice will reinforce your awakened consciousness—and this awakened consciousness is your ticket out of dissatisfaction and into the Spiritual Zone. Let's go forward on our travels holding your intention to be ready to adopt a willingness to do whatever it takes to show up in the Spiritual Zone:

Diet: eat healthfully because you love yourself
Exercise: build your body's capacity to handle more and higher frequency energy
Examine and wean yourself from unconscious thoughting
Find mental clarity

> *"Better keep yourself clean*
> *and bright; you are the*
> *window through which you must*
> *see the world."*
> GEORGE BERNARD SHAW

EXERCISES

These exercises are to help you understand that unconscious thoughts and past emotional inputs still hold reign in your physical presence on earth—your body. Bringing more conscious awareness to your body identity will help you to open your belief system. Understand that forgiveness is a tool to release the past. These exercises will prepare you experientially for the intellectual concepts that we will address in the next few chapters.

Complete the following sentences:

I forgive my parents for saying my body was

_____

_____

_____

_____

List everything that your belief system says is wrong about yourself and your body: the size, the shape, the weight:

_____

_____

_____

_____

What is your number 1 fear that keeps you from accepting that your body is perfect?

_____

_____

_____

_____

_____

✤ AFFIRMATIONS ✤

Write and speak the following affirmations, returning to reinforce ones that have particular resonance for you:

1. My body is strong, beautiful and perfect right now.
2. I accept and love my body.
3. I forgive myself for judging my body.
4. My body is vibrant and healthy.
5. I forgive myself for ever hurting my body.
6. Whatever I choose to eat is energy of love.
7. The more I love myself—the more opportunities I attract.

2

Letting Go of the Emotional Past and Choosing to Love Yourself

The practices we explored in Chapter One will give you some clarity, opening a window through old negative habits from which the light of your new life can now shine. With a continued healthier diet, more regular exercise and clear, intentional thinking, you will build your personal resources to support the happiness, love and prosperity you want to create for yourself. With this new intentionality toward how you care for your body, control your thoughts and nourish healthy emotions, the hardware is in place. It is now time to begin to clarify your picture of who you will be once you begin living in the Spiritual Zone.

True intelligence is the high spiritual power flowing through each one of us. How do we access this intelligence? *Through the heart.* Our feelings and intuitions are clear indicators of what is spiritually important to us. We must trust our hearts—*no matter what.*

Letting Go of Your Outmoded Past

Now is the time to examine what attachments to your old circumstances need to be brought to your conscious awareness so that you can release them as you journey forward into the Spiritual Zone. We don't need to invest too much attention into what it is that we have found dissatisfying in our lives, but some probing will help to identify key issues and experiences so that we can more effectively separate ourselves from them.

In the bottle breathing exercise in Chapter One, we practiced how to deal with intrusive thoughts that distract from our intention: observe them neutrally without engagement, seeing them as apart and separate from ourselves. That simple practice is the foundation for what we want to do with beliefs about our lives and ourselves and the world that no longer fit our current needs or desires.

The practices in Chapter One, when applied with regularity and ongoing mindfulness, will have the effect of bringing our negative beliefs and assumptions about ourselves into our awareness; like your old wardrobe from the 1970s doesn't fit who you are any longer, neither do many of your long-held beliefs and assumptions about who you are and what your life is like. You have first to wake up your awareness that you are still wearing the same old powder-blue polyester suit you got in 1975— it feels so familiar that you haven't realized how inappropriate it is thirty years later. The heightened awareness that results from the practices and exercises of Chapter One will help you quickly to realize that what you are wearing is no longer appropriate to the person you are today. Trading in misfitting garments and outmoded beliefs is the very act that will propel you into the Spiritual Zone.

I want to propose an exercise to you now; please approach it with lightheartedness. The point of it is to become really aware of those beliefs and situations you have adopted and constructed for yourself that no longer fit. This is not about beating yourself up—it is about creating some separation between the past and the present through your heightened awareness, your mindfulness. Imagine you are looking at old photos from the 1970s with a dear friend. It is easy for you to laugh at yourself now for choices you made back then. The powder-blue polyester suit was trendy at the time—you were stylin'! But now you have changed—it doesn't fit who you are today.

So keep it lighthearted. Enter into this exercise with an attitude of self-forgiveness. Be ready to forgive anything you perceive as once appropriate, but no longer so. The point is to create some conscious distance between your contemporary self who is about to undertake a journey to the Spiritual Zone and aspects of your life that simply don't fit who you are any longer.

Find a quiet, private place where you can be comfortable and uninterrupted for half an hour. Bring a pen or pencil and five sheets of paper.

You are going to take an inventory of your beliefs about your life, identifying all the powder-blue polyester suits that no longer fit your twenty-first-century self.

Let's begin. Freely list anything that comes up for you. Nothing is too petty or too big. If it comes up, it comes up for a reason, so put it on your list. Be as specific as you can without getting distracted from your task. You are only making a list, not writing paragraphs or an essay. Start at the center: what are your outmoded beliefs about yourself? Did you once decide that you are ugly and undeserving of love? Did you decide you have bad hair, or that you are bad at math? Poor at directions? Did you decide your sister is prettier than you are or your brother is smarter? Did you decide at some point in your past that you are weak or weak-willed? Did you decide that sexual intimacy was too dangerous for you? That you aren't deserving of a considerate, fabulous lover? That you just plain aren't good enough? Did you tell yourself that you can't resist chocolate? Or cigarettes? That you are shy? That you'll always be heavyset? That you don't easily relate to other people? That you are afraid of flying? Keep going. List any self-belief that no longer serves your picture of who you are in the Spiritual Zone. You wouldn't want to wear your clichéd old wardrobe in chic Rome, would you?

Now take a new sheet of paper and begin working outward from your self. Consider your family and your primary relationships. What are your outmoded beliefs in relation to them? Did you decide once upon a time that they didn't love you and that it was somehow your fault? That you would never be as financially successful as your father? That you would never be as selflessly generous as your mother? That you would never be as kind as your grandmother? How might you have limited yourself with beliefs you have adopted in relation to your family and your intimates? Where have you compared yourself unnecessarily to a loved one and come up short? Add to your list. If something comes up for you, don't judge it—just write it down.

Now widen the circle with a fresh piece of paper. What outmoded beliefs do you hold about yourself in relationship to your broader community—your coworkers or colleagues, your church, your neighbors and townsfolk? What roles have you been playing that no longer fit?

Have you decided to be the perky one at your office in order to earn acceptance? The dingbat? Did you decide you have to be aloof to get respect? Have you tried to build yourself up by making judgments about others? What false expression have you adopted to give yourself a sense of security? Are you trying to make a statement about yourself by the car that you drive? By other ways that you spend money? Are these accessories serving who you are now? Get current by listing everything that doesn't fit. Be kind and ready to forgive yourself; simply use your clarity and perspective to put words on paper. No one will read this but you.

Now, using a new piece of paper, expand the circle yet again—this time to the whole world. What things had you once decided that now no longer fit? Can you identify unconscious racial judgments that might have belonged to a grandparent or a teacher but are not serving who you want to be now? Did you adopt assumptions about whole countries or regions of the world that now preclude you from valuing and enjoying the inhabitants of those regions as unique individuals? Did you decide that the world is a dangerous or hostile place? Have you attached blame to people for the transgressions of their ancestors? You get the idea. Go on. Do you hold inappropriate positive generalizations? Do you think Italians are sexier than you'll ever be?

Now, take another piece of paper. What have you decided about the Universe? Have you believed that it is an unsafe place? That you are an unwelcome intruder? That you have committed transgressions during your life that make you an undeserving participant in all the joy and prosperity that the Universe has to offer? On some level, did you decide that love, all-abiding, omnipotent love, is outside your reach? That something you have said or done or been has disqualified you from the source of Universal love and light?

Consider your beliefs about your relationships to and your assumptions about *anything and everything*. Identify all those beliefs you are ready to release and let them flow onto your paper: self, family, community, world, Universe. Let your pen flow. Don't worry about how they sound, how they're written—no one but you will ever read this piece of paper. Purge yourself of all you would like to be rid of, all the baggage that you at one time or other decided—consciously or unconsciously—

that you were bound to carry through life. You are going to lighten up in order to travel to the Spiritual Zone. All these outmoded assumptions have made you too heavy for the flight.

So take a half hour and make your list. Don't worry about forgetting something. You can do this exercise again and again. Don't hesitate to write something down. If it came up for you during your examination of the circles that contain your life, it arose rightfully. List it.

Time yourself. One half hour. Then come back.

Do you feel lighter already? Now find a place where you can be alone, maybe outside. Bring some matches and a deep pot, or find a fireproof surface—your fireplace or barbecue or driveway or patio. You are going to enact a little ritual. Speak out loud to yourself. "I release myself from these beliefs that no longer serve the spiritual intent of my life. I forgive myself for having held these beliefs."

Read out loud your initial list of the first circle: the beliefs you had held about yourself. Take your time with each item and feel yourself consciously separating from it. Take as long as you need to, but don't get distracted from your task. Now, without dwelling on any of your items, scrunch up and light this page, stating once again: "I release myself from these beliefs that no longer serve the spiritual intent of my life. I forgive myself for having held these beliefs." Observe as the old causes of your worry and dissatisfaction go up in smoke. You have been released from your outmoded beliefs about yourself. *Believe this.*

Now repeat this ritual with each of your four remaining lists. Read and burn your lists of outmoded beliefs about your family, your community, the world and the Universe, repeating after each one: "I release myself from these beliefs that no longer serve the spiritual intent of my life. I forgive myself for having held these beliefs."

After you have completed all five, sit quietly and take a deep breath. Feel yourself lighter and unburdened. Recognize the energy that is now available to you that had previously been consumed holding these old beliefs. Know that you are ready to fly. If you have any of yesteryear's clothes in your closet, now is the time to get rid of them as well. You must make room for the expanse of your new life in the Spiritual Zone.

This can be an ongoing practice as your consciousness grows

continually more awake. Clarity is power. The more consciousness you bring to your belief systems, the more power you have to change them in order to create the life that you want. Continue to practice mindful observation of your beliefs and assumptions. Make this a lifelong practice of reviewing and renewing your belief constructs. Objectify outmoded beliefs by setting them apart from your contemporary self—you can do this at first by recreating the list-and-burn ritual; as the practice evolves, you will be able to complete the same objectifying effect by doing the ritual mentally. With practice, you will be able to eliminate all ill-fitting and outmoded beliefs at the very moment you identify them. The result will be that you have a more fluid, more contemporary, more enabling, more alive life.

Act on your new belief systems. If you no longer believe that you'll inevitably go back to being fat, then clear out your closet and get rid of your fat clothes—otherwise they still sit in your life as an end result. As long as you hold on to them you hold on to the belief that you will need them—and you will! Keeping them is a creative act that guarantees fatness. Be clear and be thorough in your follow-through.

Archetypes

In my work with private clients examining their self-beliefs, I have come to discover that many people have adopted overarching identities that encompass numerous subsystems of beliefs. It sometimes helps me to ask them: "What archetypal role are you playing?" I have found several common archetypes, a few of which I will list for you here because they might help you in your ongoing self-examination:

THE SAVIOR

These people are trying to be Mother Teresa. This is not to say that people cannot genuinely have the impulse to help others—certainly Mother Teresa did! But many people have taken up the mistaken belief that they are undeserving (of love, intimacy, success, happiness, prosperity) and only by saving others can they increase their deserving-ness. They can't. They are only feeding the mistaken belief at the core of their behavior—their undeservingness. This is what needs to be objectified and released.

THE SETTLER

This type, like the Savior, grows around an all-consuming belief in their own undeservingness. Settlers think so little of themselves that they will always settle for what someone else wants or chooses. They may think this is generosity that will increase their deservingness, but it is only selfishness masquerading as generosity. Settlers are subordinating their unlimited spiritual life plan to their ego's restricted self-image.

THE EXECUTIVE

I use this title to identify people who have an overarching need to con-trol. This comes from a chronic distrust that they are safe in their lives—a misbelief that they adopted somewhere in their pasts. It must be released in order to enter into the Spiritual Zone. There is no positive result to those who hope to build themselves up by controlling others.

THE QUEEN

This type, like the Executive, is a manifestation of comprehensive dis-trust in others. The Queen has set herself apart from others in social iso-lation, based on the mistaken belief that she is somehow "better" than others. In fact, she has separated herself from opportunities to love and be loved.

THE MACHO GUY

Like all these narrow archetypes, this type is also fear-based. The Macho Guy hopes to protect himself from vulnerable, intimate contact by trying to be "better" (more, bigger, stronger, faster, richer) than others.

Some of my clients, while not identifying with a particular archetype themselves, find that they are continually getting involved with a particular archetype. One client of mine—I'll call her Elena—keeps getting involved with hurtful, handsome, younger men. She gets so caught up in the web of magnetic sexual energy that all her capacities for judging what is good for her go out the window. Intellectually, she knows it isn't good for her to keep pursuing these shallow involvements—but she's not used to being treated nicely. I am coaching Elena to stand up for herself. Her habitual involvements are not acceptable. I tell her: Don't settle for a mediocre life!

Acting As If You Love Yourself

So how does Elena get out of her habitual pattern? There is a very simple route: *she must act as if she loves herself.* I coach Elena to act as if she loves herself—because it is a choice. What kind of man would a self-loving Elena attract and pursue? These men are likely to be kind, responsible, caring, generous—they are men who love themselves. Maybe the old sexual magnetism isn't there right up front with these men; in fact, it likely wouldn't be, because part of what Elena had found attractive in the past was the confirmation of her own undeservingness. She will have to objectify and release her long-held undeservingness so that it is no longer the organizing force in her relationships.

I want to take a moment here to talk about how your intimate relationships might be likely to change when you enter the Spiritual Zone. In my work with hundreds of clients I see this time and time again. Both men and women have a long-standing picture of the "type" they are attracted to. In most cases, this attraction comes primarily from their sexual center. Something in their past imprinted on them that "tall, dark and handsome" or "blonde, curvy and cute" was what made their blood rush. We all know the feeling: a sudden wallop to the pit of our stomach when we see "the type." Some of us only look; others instinctively pursue and get involved in another of what has become a chain of unsuccessful, unsatisfying involvements. If we don't wake up our awareness around these attractions and resulting involvements, we can spend our whole lives in pursuit of these disappointments. Many people have!

In the Spiritual Zone we will continue to be acutely aware of our "type" as they appear on our radar screen, but, with the higher consciousness that we have cultivated to reach and remain in the Zone, other discriminating parts of ourselves will voice their opinions about the prospective partner whom our sexual selves have singled out. In the Spiritual Zone our hearts will have a new and primary voice in this process of choosing intimate involvements. We will also access mental clarity through our more fully awake thinking, and come to consider a prospect in light of what we now know to be good for us.

This is not to say that we won't continue to be turned on by and attracted to our "type" in the Spiritual Zone, but we will respond to that attraction using the awakened capacities of our whole, more conscious being. In the Zone, Elena might notice how she finds herself physically attracted to a particular man, but before she acts on that attraction, as she would have in the past, she now listens to other parts of herself for their opinions. Her heart, which has been continually hurt in the past, will now weigh in loud and clear with its appropriate warnings.

Reading this, it probably sounds quite reasonable to bring our more fully conscious capacities to the hugely significant decisions about our romantic involvements. In practice, I have watched client after client find themselves befuddled by the unfamiliarity of their new romantic attractions. How many times have I heard a confused client say, "I really like this person but he's not my type"? Will came to see me about his business. He had been to one of my seminars, had gone home and for several weeks practiced some of the things we addressed in Chapter One, and now felt he was more awake and ready to implement some changes in his business life. When Will came to me that first day, he seemed happily perplexed.

Before he spoke about his business issues, he said he wanted to tell me about this woman he had met in his yoga class. He said she was beautiful, but that he wasn't especially sexually attracted to her. In fact, he thought she was older than he was, and typically he had been involved with younger women. This woman was tall and brunette, and his "type" had been shorter, athletic blondes. He had nevertheless felt drawn to this woman and had asked her to go out for tea after their class one evening. They had sat in a café and talked for nearly three hours. Throughout the conversation, Will found himself remarking what a lovely woman she was. She was kind and generous and heartful, compassionate. She represented all the qualities that he respected. Will told me that if she had asked him for anything, he would have unquestionably said yes; he would have wanted to support any need that she had. I asked Will if he felt he loved her. He said that, yes, he felt that he did love her—but he quickly added that it wasn't a sexual feeling he had for her, but more like the love he felt for his sister or a friend. Yet he had been thinking of this woman ever since, and he was perplexed. He wanted to see her again and be in her company, but she wasn't "his type," and he didn't feel sexual attraction to her.

Will's situation is a common occurrence for new arrivals to the Spiritual Zone. Many people spend their lives seeking romantic partners, but their search originates from their unconscious pathologies. Their "type" doesn't yet align with the conscious, healed person they will become in the Spiritual Zone. Instead, their attractions are driven by any number of unconscious desires. They could stem from an imprint from their childhood; I have seen only too many adult male clients who are still trying to replicate the first *Playboy* centerfold model they saw as a boy twenty or thirty or even forty years earlier. These unconscious attractions aren't always overtly sexual. A client named Louise discovered that she had spent fifteen years looking for men who would treat her as abusively as her mother had been treated when Louise was growing up; she thought "edgy" men were her type, and she had found plenty of them.

Bringing consciousness and self-love to our romantic relationships will of course change the "type" of person we become involved with. Will's confusion was due to the fact that he had previously failed to discriminate through his higher consciousness. He loved this woman in his yoga class; the attraction was from the heart—the fourth chakra. All his previous attractions had come from his sexual center—the second chakra. The whole process of entering the Spiritual Zone has the intention of realigning our own center of energetic being to the heart.

Will continued to meet with this woman. They communicated well and freely, and he was able to tell her that he loved her—that he didn't want anything from her, that the love he felt for her was its own reward. Will was attuned to unconditional love. This is the true sustaining source of the Universe. Through his mindful practices, Will had attuned himself to the Spiritual Zone. He found he loved the woman from his yoga class—and he found he loved himself. His attractions had shifted from being unconscious and pathological to being an expression of his own self-love.

So think about this: How do those who love themselves behave in the world? How would you behave if you truly loved yourself? Would you be more relaxed? More trusting? Less tricky and manipulative? Kinder to others? More generous? More loving? Would you establish clear, firm boundaries for yourself so that you could ensure that you live in an environment that is good for you? Would you be more honest and truthful? More fearless? More centered in your heart?

Have you ever noticed that there are people you meet, or those already in your life, who radiate a certain energy? There is something about these people that attracts our attention. We feel drawn to them or inspired by them—and we're not sure why. They have a certain charisma that we find ourselves yearning for. There is a peace and contentment about them, an inner joy they seem to experience, no matter where they are, who they are with, or what is going on around them. They walk through with unshakable confidence and unfaltering optimism, and we wonder where it comes from. Each of these radiant people has something in common: *they love themselves.* Regardless of how anyone else has ever felt about them, they have chosen to love themselves. The joy and confidence we sense from them are reflections of this self-love. Because they love themselves, they attract success in relationships, in their work, and in every other aspect of their lives. They give to themselves everything they would give to a dear loved one.

When you choose to love yourself, you are affirming your own greatness. You're energetically saying to the Universe: "I choose to hold myself in loving regard as I would hold a loved one in such regard. I am loveable. I deserve happiness. I deserve success. I deserve love." How you treat yourself directs other individuals and the entire Universe exactly how you wish to be treated in life. If you choose to love yourself, others will be drawn to "love you back." If you love yourself, the Universe will mirror this love back to you.

You can begin by simply saying, "I love myself." Say it all the time, especially when you feel the least like saying it, when you feel it's untrue or when you feel you don't deserve to love yourself. By saying it in these moments, you open to the possibility of it. We *decide* to love ourselves; it is a choice—a simple yet profound choice with miraculous results.

If you feel hesitant about saying you love yourself, chances are you're contemplating a mental list of all the reasons you shouldn't or don't deserve that love. Release all the voices coming up with excuses for why you can't love yourself. Let these voices and excuses go, just like you let distracting thoughts go in your bottle breathing practice. Let the negative voices go and act as if you love yourself. Move forward. Decide to be the kind of person who radiates light, walking through life with an unshakable inner joy and confidence.

It begins with your intention. Say to yourself, "I love myself," and let the rest go. Do you feel the shift in energy when you say these three words? When you think these three words? It is happening. Your energy is shifting each time you say or think, "I love myself." This practice is releasing baggage that was never yours to begin with; it is opening spaces, making room for happiness and success, for access to all the infinite love that the Universe has to offer.

As you continue to say, "I love myself," the color of your energy shifts. It is becoming brighter and more vibrant. You begin to radiate the light you've seen in others, the light you've been attracted to. You have had self-love all along; you only needed to act as if you love yourself to remind yourself of this truth. Keep saying it and watch your life shift. Love is the creative, healing energy of the Universe. By invoking love into your life, the impossible becomes possible, the complicated becomes simple, confusion becomes clarity. It's a simple choice, a decision. You make thousands of decisions every day. Why shouldn't you make this one? The decision to say, "I love myself," will absolutely change your life. It is your passport to the Spiritual Zone.

EXERCISES

These exercises will assist you in eliminating behavior patterns that you no longer want in your life. Although we have examined patterns in relationships, the same technique can be applied to other areas.

Make a list of patterns that seem to recur in each of these areas:
• Health situations
• Money situations
• Relationships
• Job situations

Note that your thoughts and beliefs can also be handed down from your parents or family. Example: my mother was the dominant one in our family relationship, and my wife is now the dominant one in mine. Look at the immediate family of your childhood and see if its patterns are reflected in your immediate family of today.

You can readjust your situation, with boundaries or letting go, or asking yourself the question: Is this situation moving me backwards, standing still or forwards? Based on your answer, make your choice to correct the situation by letting go of the unconscious assumptions you have been holding, setting boundaries that will keep you on track, and keeping your focus on the end result of what it is that you want. You do not need to micromanage every step between where you are and where you want to be. By identifying the truth of where you are and keeping focused on where you want to be, you have established a Spiritual Zone in which the creative forces of the Universe will act to connect the two.

List the things that you would like to do some day.

_____

_____

_____

_____

List the ways in which you value yourself over money, things and accomplishments:

_____

_____

_____

_____

Be aware that in letting go of old beliefs your intention is to have clarity in what you really want.

Writing these old beliefs is a way of cleansing. Now let's replace these old patterns by saying: "I no longer accept these beliefs and let go now!"

🍂 AFFIRMATIONS 🍂

1. I give myself permission to live and be abundant.
2. I believe in success and happiness.
3. I break all agreements within my soul memory that limit me.
4. I am free to be joyous and happy.
5. I let my past experiences go. They have no power over me.
6. I am free to experience only my greatest love with myself, my relationships and life.
7. I only accept love in my life.
8. The more I am love, the more I enjoy each moment.

3

Practicing Forgiveness to Have the Love You Deserve

Imagine an incident with a loved one where one of you hurt the other through some words or actions. This incident left your relationship out of sorts until the offending party apologized and the aggrieved party offered forgiveness. It was the act of forgiveness—not the apology—that restored unity to the relationship. Forgiveness has the unique power to heal separations. Not only can it heal a temporary rift between you and a loved one, it can heal the illusion that you are separate from your infinite spiritual self. Forgiveness can restore you to the Spiritual Zone, and to the experience of abundant love.

This is the truth: there is nothing you have ever been or done that is unforgivable. Nothing. Believe this and you will change your life. Stop and take this in, then feel your body relax: *there is nothing you have ever been or done that is unforgivable.*

Imagine you are a parent of a young child; there is nothing your two- or three-year-old child could do that you wouldn't forgive—nothing! Of course you would forgive him any transgression; not forgiving him seems ridiculous! You may not forgive the behavior, but you would certainly forgive your child. You know it is the nature of a three-year-old child to make mistakes; you easily understand this. Well, it is the nature of the adult human being to make mistakes as well. *This is how we learn.* If we were perfect beings, we wouldn't have needed to make this visit to planet Earth.

Like you are so unquestionably ready to forgive the mistakes and transgressions of your three-year-old child, so must you be prepared to forgive yourself. The acceptance of the possibility of your own forgiveness is your way out of your fearful illusions of separation and lack and your way into the Spiritual Zone, where you will have the truly abundant life that you want. Forgiveness is the difference between seeing yourself as an isolated ego-mind regulating scarcity and as a spiritual being enjoying perfect abundance. It is the bridge between seeing yourself as unworthy and incomplete and seeing yourself as loving, strong and in unity with the source of all love and light. Forgiveness corrects your very human mistake of identifying with the limited mind and realigns you with the unlimited spiritual being you truly are. You will find that as you release your tight hold on your perceived limits, you will relax into the ready flow of your abundant spirituality.

Healing Separation

You mustn't confuse forgiveness of others as a moral issue about generosity, self-sacrifice and big-heartedness; it is, rather, a tremendous, self-sustaining gift from yourself to yourself. Forgiveness requires that you give up all judgment, and in giving up judgment you become free to give up separation. While you may tell yourself that judgment is about others, in fact all judgment is directed at the self because in the Spiritual Zone we are all connected to one self where there is no "other." "Other" is only a perception of the ego, an illusion of the separated self. Judgment of others is motivated only by your own perceived unworthiness to be at one with them. Our egos subscribe to the illusion of separation from others as a means to reinforce our guilty perception of our separateness from the source.

In truth, you were given everything you will ever need or want at conception. Forgiving—giving up—your mistaken belief in separation separates your identity from the very limited assumptions of your ego and returns you to the wholeness—*and the holiness*—of the Spiritual Zone. In the acceptance of your truth as a spiritual being, you will find yourself aligned and at one with the whole of creation—and with such previously elusive ideals as real love, joy, prosperity, creativity and peace.

The more we forgive—give up—the false perception that we are separate, isolated egos, the more access we have to the abundance of life in the Spiritual Zone. Assessing how much you have—or don't have—of what you want in life will help you to see where you have blocks and where you can benefit from more self-forgiveness.

A Case Study

Our relationships are an especially clear measure of our self-worth. Consider the experience of Carol, an extremely successful business-woman who had adopted the archetype of the Savior, as I wrote about in Chapter Two. Carol had established a pattern of saving men—particu-larly men who could hold on to jobs for only a short time. Carol, think-ing she was Mother Teresa, always had to bail them out, financially and emotionally. This repeated pattern was draining, both to her bank account and to her spirit. Looking at this pattern on a deeper level, Carol finally saw that she was repeatedly choosing men she could control. She thought she had to control her relationships because she was acting as a valve regulating the perceived scarcity identified by her limited self-worth.

Carol would always pay for everything for her men. They quickly took her for granted, never acknowledging that she was special and fan-tastic. These relationships were based on false ego-perceptions, so there was never the opportunity for Carol and her partners to be present together in the truth of the Spiritual Zone. Carol was always giving, giv-ing, giving, and never receiving—except for receiving her partners' bills, liabilities and constant needs.

This was her pattern with her recent partner, David. David was com-pletely unaware of the spiritual being he was in truth, and Carol, also unaware, was obsessed with controlling him. Unlike a healthy, balanced partnership that flows with love and support, this partnership was built on entwined, needy illusions. Carol would always provide the good life for David—travel, clothes, gifts, cards, attention—but her true motivation was to control him. The truth was, she needed to control him in order to fill her self-identified lack: her twisted logic told her that if David was her partner, she must be okay. In truth, control opposes healing; Carol's self-limiting delusions could only be healed through forgiveness.

David was also separated from the truth. He, too, was operating from the tight limits of his mind, withholding and protecting his illusions of scarcity. He never acknowledged the greatness of Carol; in his delusion, that would mean less greatness for himself. His twisted logic told him that if he told Carol she was great she would leave him for someone more deserving. David's mistaken belief was that there was never enough, particularly never enough money, or help. Outside the Spiritual Zone, he was living apart from the flow of the Universal source, so he had no real power. He was always looking to siphon off someone else's power to prop him up or bail him out. He was looking for the impossible.

One day, something unusual happened to Carol. She'd been having serious problems with David. They were fighting. He was drinking, turning to drugs, verbally abusing her. Carol kept going back for more because she still believed she could control him. She thought that if she provided for David's needs, he would love her and his love would give her value; this was Carol's delusion, that our value can be earned or secured by outside circumstances.

They lived together. Carol often went out with friends after work so that she would not have to be at home with David. This particular evening, one of the friends had invited a man named John to join them. Carol was so mesmerized by John she could hardly speak. What was this compelling energy? It was a soul-level recognition. John asked for her phone number; Carol hesitated. Her situation with David seemed like a nightmare, and she needed something else. She made a decision in that moment to follow her attraction, and she gave John her number. This was her healing instant: Carol had relinquished control. She had forgiven (given up) her separation from the Spiritual Zone by listening to her intuition and taking action. She immediately got the message that John would be her soul mate, her friend and, later, her husband.

When Carol met John a week later for coffee, the intense energy between them was like nothing she had ever experienced. It was truth, unfolding right before her.

Forgiving Illusions

There is an old saying: "The truth will set you free." *This is a fact.* By forgiving yourself of your illusions of alienation and lack, you free yourself of your mistaken separate identity and realign yourself with the infinite resources of the Spiritual Zone. This is true freedom—from lack, from constraint, from all forms of settling for less than you deserve. There is nothing you have ever been or done that is unforgivable. By accepting this truth and living in the truth of who you are *right now,* there is an alignment, a healing, a click that occurs. You return to your spiritual identity. In actuality, you realize that you have been in the Spiritual Zone all along. The veil of your illusion of separation is lifted. Things fall into place. You fall into grace. The life you want is here now, yours for the asking, only a click away.

Carol was floating with the high of her connection with John in truth. John acknowledged her, showered her with attention, sent her birthday flowers and a silver key chain with the note, "Celebrate your life!" David found out about the gifts and panicked that Carol might leave him. He promised her that he would change, that he'd go into therapy and get help for his substance abuse. David made all the promises, but he wasn't coming from a place of truth or love; he was coming from fear of scarcity, of losing his meal ticket. Carol, still the Savior, again bought into this illusion because she wasn't yet ready to give up control. She reinvested in the mistake of her unworthiness—she felt she didn't deserve to be in truth with John at that moment. She chose instead to hope things would improve with David.

Very few of us truly practice looking at ourselves in the present. We hope for future accomplishments, dread future mistakes. We bask in our past accomplishments and wallow in past disappointments. We avoid looking at ourselves *right now,* the only true place, the only true opportunity to choose who we will be in this world and what we want for ourselves. The basking and wallowing and anticipating are judgments against who we think we are right now. We tell ourselves, "In the future I'll be better," or "I've done so poorly in the past, I'm no good . . ." This is a game we play, an illusion we harbor, a dream we dream in order to enforce our separation from the Spiritual Zone. Why do we do this? Because we are not awake. Because we have fallen into identifying with our little separate minds instead of our infinite spirits. Why? Because we have forgotten the true reality of our wholeness and adopted the dream/illusion/false reality of our separateness. Our egos fight for sovereignty over our lives by reinforcing this illusion of separation with continuous judgment and guilt. Forgiveness is the only way back to truth.

When Carol told John of her decision to try again with David, John released her with love and told her he wished the best for her and David. John, already living in the Spiritual Zone, was coming from a place of truth. He trusted the abundant Universe to give him what he needed. If indeed Carol needed to be with David, John would accept that.

Truth enables true closeness with others, authentic spiritual union. We long for intimacy in our lives but fail to live in the only place where intimacy resides, the true here and now. Carol held on to her illusions about herself and David; she hung on to her projection that if she just hung in there, she might have fulfillment in the future. John released her with love—and his experience of both Carol and her decision was loving.

Soon David reverted to his old behaviors. He could never tell the truth, could never approach Carol from a place of pure love. Carol, having had that brief visit to the Spiritual Zone with John as her traveling companion, quickly realized she needed truth. She needed to be her true self. She chose to become open, honest and trusting. She asked David to move out of their home, and her life quickly changed. She and John bonded as friends and as soul mates. The truth brought them the utmost joy, infinite joy. They are now married and continue to give and receive love on all levels in the harmony of a committed, balanced, spiritual partnership lived fully in the Spiritual Zone.

The Honest Truth

Truth gives us access to all the gifts of creation—*right now.* We long for prosperity (by which I mean an abundance of all that is good) in our lives, but separated from truth our limited minds hold us as undeserving and separate. If our jealous, separated minds judge others we perceive as prosperous, we distance ourselves not only from them but also from prosperity itself, which, in the Spiritual Zone, is our birthright as well as theirs. Accepting our truth is the portal to the life we want.

The honest truth is you have everything and everyone that you want right now. Carol experienced that healing instant of trusting that John would be good for her. The trick is to realize that you are not who your limited ego thinks you are. In her moment of clarity with John, Carol saw that she needn't be concerned with controlling men in order to have the facade of a love relationship. She awoke to the realization that she wasn't who she had thought she was. Carol's own spirituality reached out to her through John's clarity and assured her that she could let go and trust; and from that surrendered place, she could experience true love.

Remember, nothing you have ever been or done is unforgivable. Carol thought she was lonely and needy and longing and undeserving, but she'd made a mistake about her identity. A mistake, that's all, a mistake like a three-year-old child makes. All mistakes are correctable.

Have you made this same mistake of identifying with your limited mind, with your self-protecting ego who lives outside the Spiritual Zone? Are you willing to recognize that this is a mistake, forgive it and embrace your true, spiritual self? You are not who you thought you were. In truth, you are a spiritual being. You are the spirituality experiencing itself in human form, in the unique and extraordinary circumstances and opportunities of your particular human life. If you use forgiveness to release your illusions and accept this truth right now and in every moment, you will find yourself at one with your every desire. You will feel no lack. You will feel yourself relax. By aligning with your truth, no matter what, you will be fulfilled in the flow of the Spiritual Zone.

My Story Before the Zone

Not so very long ago, I was in a toxic relationship at work. At the time, it felt quite normal because I didn't know anything different. I didn't know I deserved any better. I was lost, both within myself and within the situation of my job.

Not unlike Carol, I had adopted the role of the Savior in my relationship with my boss, a role that I then thought was noble and generous and good. If it was good enough for Mother Teresa, it was good enough for me. I operated under the illusion that I was making a magnanimous contribution by taking care of my employer. I truly made him look good, always taking the initiative, always doing the work, always going out of my way to acknowledge him. For all my hard work, I got no appreciation. In my heart, I felt there was something wrong with this picture, but I told myself the solution was to try harder, to be more selfless, to take better care of my boss, to work harder at being a better Savior in general, to be a better people pleaser. In truth, I wasn't being generous and considerate; I was fearful and controlling. I was working increasingly hard in order to deny my unconscious assumption that I didn't deserve this job, but I was still operating under that basic assumption. I was pouring my energy into a black hole of impossible need.

I had to go through a lot of pain and anger finally to see the truth that my boss had a problem with drug addiction. I never knew what to expect when I arrived at work each day. Things would be missing, hocked at the pawnshop to pay for his latest drug score. When I asked questions, a major scene would ensue, as if it were my fault. I only wanted to help! I told myself that things would get better, that I just had to be more helpful, to be more supportive—because clearly my boss needed me.

I was exhausted. I felt a cavernous emptiness inside. I began eating like crazy and quickly gained thirty pounds. I felt terrible. I needed to do something, but I didn't know what. Then I heard about a masters swim team. I'd always been a competitive swimmer growing up—the water and the camaraderie of the sport had always balanced me. I joined the team and started to spend time with my teammates, traveling to swim meets at least twice a month. I grew healthier, both physically from the workouts and emotionally from the meditative time spent in the water and from the time spent in the company of my emotionally healthy teammates. The more I immersed myself in their positive energy, the more I began to trust that my work situation was not good for me.

When you change the type of people you spend time with, your energy shifts. *Living around truth will require you to live in truth.* I began to trust that I would be okay if I were to walk away from my job. I traveled to a national championship masters swimming meet in Indiana and broke two world records! From the tremendous high of this personal accomplishment, I returned to work to find that half the office equipment—the fax, the computer, the VCR and other items—was gone! My boss had needed some money for getting high. That was the end. I put my foot down and quit.

I began doing yoga and became clearer. Once I started to clean the house of all my dysfunctional entanglements, I began to see that the problem had not only been my boss—the problem had also been my trying to control the situation. The truth was, I hadn't believed that I was enough—good enough, capable enough, smart enough, caring enough, aligned enough—to deserve a healthy work relationship. I was still holding a perception of myself as an isolated ego, separate from the source; and, because I was separate, I felt unworthy and undeserving—of care, of appreciation, of a prosperous, healthy work situation.

Choosing the Zone

I now see that all our situations, good and bad, are unique opportunities to see ourselves and awaken to a higher level of consciousness. Every experience is an opportunity to choose the Spiritual Zone. As toxic as this particular work relationship was for me, it was a great opportunity to see my mistaken perceptions about myself. In this regard, this difficult and unsatisfying job was a tremendous gift: it woke me up to all the false assumptions I had made about myself, all the illusions I had adopted. I had fooled myself into thinking I could improve my self-worth by being a caretaker. I had pretended my caretaking was about generosity and consideration and service, when in fact it was a mechanism I had constructed to fool myself into feeling needed, and therefore deserving of the things I wanted in life. In truth, I *am* deserving. We are all deserving. This is our birthright as inhabitants of the Spiritual Zone. We are worthy of a healthy work environment. We *are* worthy of investing in ourselves. We deserve to feel good, and we deserve to do things that make us feel good. How do I know this? I trust. I listen to my heart and not my mind, to my spiritual self and not my ego. I know that all my pain and compromises came from a mistaken, ego-driven belief that I was separate and undeserving.

How do we heal that false belief? Forgiveness. Nothing we have ever been or done is unforgivable. I forgave—gave up—this false belief and then leaned on trust to act as if I were at one with spirit. I created a new picture of my reality, leaving behind the separate, caretaking self who felt undeserving of the flow of abundance. I chose instead a new self at one with spirit and entitled to all the infinite and loving gifts of creation.

When we are coming from truth, from higher consciousness, our desires change, and we have a completely different relationship to them. In the Spiritual Zone we trust that our desires are healthy and honorable. There is no delusional competition telling me that my desires can only be met at the exclusion of someone else's. We do not have to settle for compromised situations that reflect our unworthiness. We can seek to fulfill our true desires directly, with love and without guilt that our gain will cause anyone else loss. By embracing opportunities to fulfill our true selves, we are honoring the One True Self. In the Spiritual Zone, aligned with the whole, we know that my true desires are achieved without cost to anyone else—because in truth there is no scarcity or lack. My gain is your gain. Your gain is my gain, for in truth we are all one. In this truth we bring a whole different self to all our situations and relationships and undertakings. We are no longer defending our separateness; instead, we act in all decisions toward union. The result is a deeply satisfying experience of flow. This is the nature of life in the Zone.

The Shift

At this time of transition into the higher consciousness of the heart center, many of us are fractured. Our egos and minds—which pride themselves on having kept us safe and alive up until now—have an impossible task of letting go and trusting that we will be safe in the hands of our spirituality. By their very nature, and because they are attackers themselves, our egos see the world as an unsafe place, requiring a keen defense and constant vigilance against attack in all forms at all times. Our egos don't trust our spiritual selves to be able to defend successfully against attack, because they don't trust even the idea of spirituality; they are, by their very nature, separated from our spirituality. They are also separated from truth.

We are, right now, in a major shift in human consciousness. All humanity is stepping out of darkness and into the light of the Spiritual Zone. For thousands of years, people have been living in their defensive egos, separate from spirit and separate from truth. Now we are beginning to realize that in truth, we are all spiritual beings. We are all one spiritual being. Our home is the Zone. Our egos, however, will never accept this; they are innately separate, defensive constructs, and as such unable to trust. Do we identify with them, as we have habitually and historically done, or do we listen to the call and acknowledge and accept our true spiritual selves? This is the grand struggle of our present era. Do we step into the Zone, or do we remain in illusion? Our journey will inevitably lead to our eventual transcendence, for truth always overcomes illusion. But just because it is inevitable doesn't mean we always make it easy on ourselves.

I have a client named Sarah, who is very spiritual, a yoga teacher, a loving mate and loving mother to two young children. Sarah decided recently that her children, now in school, were old enough that she could go back to work full-time. Although she had never been a professional teacher before, she felt called to become a kindergarten teacher; she felt that today's young children, whose families—and culture—are struggling with this transition into heart and spirit, were calling to her to guide them in this journey. Sarah strongly believes that children must be encouraged and supported in existing in their truth as spiritual beings.

While Sarah is an extremely capable woman, she had never taught young children before, except as a mother. She knew she wanted to work in the service of spirit, so she simply followed her internal voice that teaching was what she was meant to do at this time. Sarah applied to be a kindergarten assistant in two different urban schools—and was promptly offered lead-teacher positions by both schools. Sarah found this surprising and flattering—and somewhat overwhelming. She had very little experience and only a minimum of training, but miracles happen in the Spiritual Zone, where we stand in the truth of who we are. When you commit to your spirituality, your life can take immediate and radical shifts. Sarah ultimately accepted one of the lead-teacher positions because the school administrators said they badly needed her and because she felt the students in this particular kindergarten class had called out to her to come and be their guide.

When we consciously identify with our truth as spiritual beings, our lives can change abruptly—but this is no guarantee that our egos will go along docilely with the changes. Teaching in an urban, state school setting, Sarah found her class populated with challenging, high-needs students. While her colleagues on the faculty may have had more training and teaching experience, they were all deeply entrenched in the challenges of their own classrooms. The result was that Sarah found herself as an inexperienced teacher in an exceptionally demanding situation without the support of others—all of which sent her protective ego into overdrive. Judgment kicked in, telling her that her colleagues were at fault for not helping her, that the school had lost touch with its vision, that she was the wrong person for her position, that she had been a fool to take the job. She experienced all sorts of competence anxiety, questioned whether she had made a big mistake and contemplated quitting. She came home crying every afternoon and dreaded the return to work each morning, fearful that she would be unable to meet her students' needs.

As this went on for several months, Sarah got more and more run down, exhausted and overwhelmed. By the time she came to talk with me about her circumstances, she looked extremely tired, pale and surprisingly older; she was holding tremendous tension in her body. The stress of her circumstances had taken such a big toll that she told me that she felt she was dying.

In fact, Sarah *was* dying. She was in the death throes of her ego. She had put herself in a situation where there was no room for ambivalence about whether she could be her true spiritual self. There was absolutely no way her ego could manage the demands of her circumstances— which required love, trust, surrender and all kinds of help from her spiritual capacities. She absolutely had to surrender to her unlimited spirit in order to survive and succeed in meeting the needs of her class of young spiritual—and spirited—children. For her to do this felt like death to her ego; it was certainly the death of her ego's sovereignty. To the degree that Sarah herself was still identified with her ego, she felt that she was dying—physically dying. She might have, too. The ego would readily take her body along with it rather than relinquish control to her spirit. Not that Sarah was overtly suicidal, but she found herself having close calls while driving, and she nearly blew up her kitchen by turning on her gas oven but forgetting to light it. Where higher consciousness is the realm of spirit, the unconscious is subject to the agendas of ego—and Sarah's ego wasn't letting go easily.

Sarah and I have known each other a long time and we have a deep spiritual connection, so when we're together Sarah naturally gravitates toward her spiritual identity. From this place she could see that the death of the ego is only an illusion. In truth, the ego is itself an illusion—a false self, separate from our true spiritual nature. In truth, death is also an illusion, for our spirit never dies. Our spirit is infinite. In our connected conversations, Sarah was able to see that fear and anxiety—the manipulative tools of the ego—were using the challenges of her circumstances to attempt to lure her away from her confidence in her true spiritual identity. In the connection of our two spirits, she could feel the union with all things that is the truth in the Spiritual Zone. This is atonement—*at-one-ment*—the natural result of a total commitment to the truth.

Through atonement, Sarah could free herself from the mistake of listening to her ego judgments telling her she was incompetent, a failure, a pretender, a stupid person to think she could be a teacher. From within the Spiritual Zone, Sarah opens herself to infinite assistance: from her guides and angels, from her students' guides and angels, from the infinite resources of the Universal source. In the Zone, she is available to experience miracles. In the Zone, she is no longer an isolated woman in an isolated classroom desperately attempting to meet a challenging situation with book-learned processes and classroom management techniques. In the Zone, aligned with truth, Sarah is a spiritual being connecting with her kindergarten class of spiritual beings in the one source that is their common home. As long as she is tuned in to her true identity as a spiritual being, Sarah is no longer separate from truth, from her colleagues or from the children themselves. In the flow of her own truth, Sarah has infinite capacity, competence and support. It is the spiritual being of Sarah whom her children were calling to be their teacher; when she meets them at this level, the entire consciousness of the Universe conspires to help her give her children exactly what they need, exactly how and exactly when they need it. If she gets overwhelmed and loses her contact with the Spiritual Zone, every moment is a struggle and a lonely challenge.

In truth, we are never alone. In truth, we have the incomprehensible, infinite support of the entire Universe. While we may not all find ourselves in the classroom like Sarah, we are all, by example, teachers of truth. Our true mission is to live our lives in such a way as to demonstrate always that we are loving spiritual beings. In doing so, we are models of harmony, peace, prosperity, abundance, competence, confidence, commitment, compassion, joy, love and light. By embracing the truth of ourselves as spiritual beings living in the Spiritual Zone, we readily forgive our past mistakes and align ourselves to receive the spiritual gifts of the Universe. As fountains of the source, these gifts flow through us, to our particular class of students if we are teachers like Sarah, and to all with whom we come in contact.

Once we have identified what it is that we want, it is important to take a good look at the things that might be standing in our way. Where are we holding on to anger, resentments, self-judgment and the judgment of others, the residue of belief systems we have inherited or outgrown? We need to find our quiet place, call upon truth to identify the places where we need to let go, and then forgive ourselves and others who may have kept us from moving into our truth.

Everything, every aspect of your life, deserves scrutiny. If it's not serving you, if it's not serving who you want to be right now, then forgive your mistake and let go of it. If it's not the best, it's not for you. This can be tackled symbolically by looking at your possessions and your environment. What is that pile of papers collecting on your desk? Send them out or throw them out; they're weighing you down. Look in your closet. If there are clothes you haven't worn in six months, give them away; they're crowding you, taking up space from the new clothes that will express who you are now. Everything you surround yourself with must reflect your highest mind-set. It is there to remind you of who you are—the Infinite Spiritual Source experiencing itself through human incarnation.

Self-compromise is not noble or humble; this is part of the great fear-driven illusion. It doesn't serve your spirituality or your loved ones for you to be unhappy or dissatisfied. All compromise makes you small and denies your spirituality the opportunity to flow through you. It is time to use forgiveness to let go of old habits of thinking small and being small. Forgive yourself for having lived this mistake—and then forget about it.

How you respond to and think about life's challenges is one of the most important keys to successful living. We must first go back and acknowledge that incident in our past, or that truth about ourselves that we are uncomfortable with, and replace our self-judgments with forgiveness. We created the blueprint for our lives—so we can also uncreate, which we do through the tool of forgiveness. We must go back and retool the parts.

EXERCISES

Use the following questions to help identify the aspects and areas in your life that will benefit from forgiveness. I find writing down answers helps to bring clarity and insight.

1. What has your payoff been for choosing not to forgive?
2. Was there anything you gained by not forgiving someone or something or yourself?
3. Why can't you forgive yourself?
4. What is stopping you from forgiving others?
5. What is your payoff for holding on to resentment and anger?
6. What would you feel like if you felt love or loved all the time?
7. What is your belief and thoughts about having or living in a loving relationship with yourself and others?
8. What does the word "love" mean to you?
9. It's time to begin a new life, a new beginning. Let go of the baggage. Forgive yourself now and let go with love and accept love.

🍂 AFFIRMATIONS 🍂

Use the following affirmations to reinforce the new truths that you have identified for yourself. Choose the ones that resonate for you. Repeat them to yourself throughout the day, or write them twenty times a day for reinforcement.

1. I love myself.
2. I deserve only the best in life.
3. I forgive myself for everything.
4. I forgive my mother for everything.
5. I forgive my father for everything.
6. I forgive myself for hurting (him/her) and not loving (him/her).
7. I forgive and am released from all past relationships.
8. I am love.
9. I have love in all my relationships.
10. I am worthy of being loved and respected.
11. I am fully functional and ready to live love.
12. I am loving and powerful.
13. I give love and receive love.
14. I am worth it.
15. I expect a loving miracle every day.
16. I now allow myself to have an intimate loving relationship.

Part Two

How to Stay in the Spiritual Zone

4
Activating Your Power of Choice

The previous chapters have been about getting to the Spiritual Zone. To facilitate access, we explored some practices to awaken and revitalize and strengthen our bodies, to still our minds of random destructive thought, and to heal our hearts through forgiveness and choosing to love ourselves. In combination, these practices have the effect of lifting us out of the sleepy unconsciousness of the past and into the heightened awareness of the Spiritual Zone. Here in the Zone, we can use our access to higher consciousness to choose the lives we want for ourselves.

As we learned in earlier chapters, we can choose fear or love, undeservingness or deservingness, struggle or ease. We can choose our mates and romantic partners out of pathology and habit, or we can choose them out of the conscious clarity of what it is that we truly want for ourselves. We can choose to love ourselves—or choose not to.

Everything in life is a choice. Everything. This may sound brutal if you consider some of the tragedies many of us have had to endure, but it is nevertheless the truth. Two of my dear friends lost their baby son due to a freak accident in the delivery room. Their grief at their child's death was tremendous, devastating. But alongside their very human grief was the understanding that the spiritual being who was their child had made this choice for himself. They chose not to blame the hospital or doctor—or themselves—because, living in the Spiritual Zone, they understood that this so-very-brief incarnation was the exact destiny chosen by their child.

All of life is about choice. As spiritual beings, we make choices before we even enter into this life on earth. You have heard the word "destiny." Destiny is the plan that we made for this life as spiritual beings before we joined the forgetfulness of physical incarnation. We each come here with a plan for ourselves. We choose parents and siblings and birth order, race, gender, nationality and socioeconomic status. We set up our lives in order to maximize the lessons we need to learn and the experiences we seek to have as spiritual beings—all of which further the development of ourselves as souls.

So, choice is something we've all been doing for a long, long time. Conscious choice, on the other hand, may be very new to some of you. Back in Chapter Two, I talked about several archetypes; well, these types are living their lives as if they didn't have a choice. Settlers, for example, think they have to give choice over to someone else in life. That's only because they are asleep to the fact that they already made an early, comprehensive choice to act as Settlers. By making this sweeping choice, Settlers reduced the amount of smaller choices they have to make—it's as if they bought into a whole track of pre-programmed decisions. What does the fact that so many people are living archetypes instead of living fully conscious lives say about the human race? It says that people have been comfortable to be asleep. It says that people have been avoiding responsibility. It says that too many people are sleepwalking through life, or too eager to sign over their power to others to decide their lives for them. It says that humanity has been missing out on the Spiritual Zone.

I ask clients who come to see me, "What do you want?" Too many of them answer: "I don't know." How can you expect anything to come to you if you don't know what you want for yourself? Still, most people don't know what they want; they just vacillate among options and wander sleepily through life with nothing really happening. They're not happy, but they haven't given any real thought to what they could choose to have or do that would help to make them happy. If you don't know what you want, you're just going to float through life—you might as well go to a marina and sit on a boat.

When we go to restaurants, we don't have much trouble deciding what to order. We read the menu choices, tell our server what we want, and then sit back and fully trust that our choices will come to us exactly as we requested them. If you truly can't decide what to order, you have no business being in the restaurant—you're just taking up space. It's easy to see the absurdity of behavior in this example, yet most people behave in an equally absurd way when dealing with their very lives!

Aiming for an End Result

Think of an end result as a target. If you don't have a clearly articulated end result, you wander aimlessly and get nowhere. Setting very specific goals for an end result—with a due date—is the only way to get from here to there. Remember earlier when I talked about the importance of emptying your closet of fat clothes because by keeping them you were investing in the end result of becoming fat again and eventually needing to wear them? You must use your awakened consciousness to make the connection between every action you take and the end result that that action directs you toward. Get accustomed to asking yourself this question frequently throughout your day: Is this particular action going to support my end result? Is eating this piece of chocolate cake? Is attending this yoga class? Is spending an hour on this TV program? Is going on a date with this particular person?

We need to quiet ourselves, listen and focus on very specific goals. A singer, for example: "I will make the very best CD of my life that is really going to make my career take off, and I'm going to do it in one take on this Friday at noon." Or: "I want to be healthy and attractive at my perfect weight, and beginning right now I will only eat those foods in such quantities that support this picture of who I truly am." Be specific. In a restaurant, you don't just walk in and say, "Feed me"; you order a grilled aubergine and roasted red pepper sandwich on herb foccacia with basil aioli. Life will always serve us up some surprises—we don't need to add to the confusion by being unclear with our requests.

About four months ago, I saw a client I'll call Michael. Michael was highly trained as a marine biologist, but couldn't seem to pull his life together to get a job on his career path. He was living on his boat, drinking, out of control. The only reason he came to see me was that his girlfriend said she was going to leave him if he didn't get his life together. I told Michael he had to make the choices that are going to put him on the path of being the best marine biologist ever. I told him, "You need to go to the top. You need to contact the top person at the top company in your field—go there and knock on the door." Well, Michael did that and they said no; but then last week he got a call that they had reviewed his

CV and wanted to hire him to fill an open position. Michael was ecstatic! He was in his power.

Before he came to see me, Michael had been stuck in his indecision. Together we discovered that he was crippled by the internalized voice of his parents, who had fed him the message all his life that he would never amount to anything without their help. Michael had really bought into this, always trying to make things okay for Mommy and Daddy. His unconscious end result was to be sure that he never amounted to anything. By accepting the marine biologist job, Michael really stepped into his true power and broke the lifelong dysfunctional dependence on his parents. This act will change their relationship radically and forever. The next time Michael sees his parents, he will have to stand up to the challenge not to revert to his old pattern; he needs to know confidently that no matter what, he is in his true power. If they choose to blow him off or be angry with him—too bad! That's their issue; it's not his baggage. He can't go back to the old behavior or sabotage the new job just to make it okay for Mommy and Daddy. This is a big one for people who don't put themselves number one—they're always looking for the approval. They have to realize that their own self-approval is the only approval that matters. To put themselves first, it helps them tremendously to choose to love themselves.

Keeping Yourself in Alignment

I coached Michael on how to interact with his parents. He needs to approach them with a firm boundary. He needs to answer their criticisms by saying to them, "You know, Mom and Dad, that may be your point of view, but I know I always make the right decisions. I always get the jobs that are right for me." This way, he isn't arguing with them; he's letting them have their own idea, and then capping it off with his positive statement about his choice. In this way he enlivens the habitual, stagnant energy and takes the power back to use for his own greater good. It's a kind of aikido, the martial art where you redirect the force coming at you to use for your own intentions.

It is so interesting to see how people's parents' behavior sets them off.

As children, our parents had such tremendous power over us that it's easy for us to continue to defer to this authority as adults. You must keep yourself conscious and in alignment with your own spiritual greatness so that you can create the intentional thinking that manifests your right choices. This is how the Universe supports you. You must be a conduit of spiritual energy so that you make right choices every day. If you keep yourself in alignment with the Spiritual Zone, the Universe will support your greatness and bring you unlimited prosperity, unlimited opportunities, unlimited freedom, unlimited everything you want.

How do you keep yourself in alignment? Use the practices we explored in Chapter One. Keep your body conscious through right eating and exercise. Keep your thinking conscious through meditation and intention. Get clear and keep focused on your end result. Keep your heart conscious through an ongoing practice of forgiveness and by continually choosing to love yourself.

Sometimes it's hard! Some days we don't feel strong, we don't feel like we love ourselves; some days we don't feel good. Our old patterns have been so deeply ingrained that some days it really takes a lot of our energy to maintain the spiritual alignment. Many of our old patterns—like Michael's—come from childhood. They're so deep that they're in the very structure of our cells. As young children, we saw our parents as gods; we were wholly dependent on them and gave them tremendous power over our lives. Pleasing our parents represented survival to us. Now that we survive on our own as adults, it's time to remove that assumption from our motivation.

A Word to Parents

On the other side of this parent-child equation, we must be awake to the power we wield over our children. Acknowledging that power, we must be vigilantly conscious about our parenting choices. It is vitally important as parents that we give children positive reinforcement every day: that they are great, that they have something of value to contribute, that they are the stars in—and directors of—their own lives. It all starts in the home. Parents: you must find an hour or two a day intentionally to bond with your child so that during this focused attention the child feels like royalty. I'm not saying spoil them with toys. What they need is deep contact and acknowledgement. Tell your son, "You know, you're a great boy. I'm so proud and happy that I'm your father. I know you can do anything that you want. What would you like to do today?" By first giving them recognition and heartfelt positive encouragement, and then offering them a choice, you begin to build the foundation of their personal power. Every day, parents have tremendous opportunities to make the right choices on behalf of their children.

Parents also have the unique and precious opportunity *to heal the future* by bringing their highest consciousness to their parenting. Respectful, loving parenting that reinforces a child's greatness will enable the children who will grow up to be tomorrow's leaders to dream bigger than you or I could ever imagine. Remember, before incarnating into their physical bodies, your children planned their destinies. They chose you as their parent. They believed in your ability to parent them in such a way so that they could heal the future. This is an honor beyond all honors, and a responsibility beyond all responsibilities. This has been your choice as well; you made a spiritual choice to enter into this parent-child relationship. By choosing to love yourself you acknowledge your greatness—and your greatness is required to fulfill the destiny that you planned for yourself.

Dreaming Your Choices into Reality

Dreams do come true. Consider my client, Annie. When she was a child she was living in another country. She was parentless and lived in an orphanage. She kept dreaming, looking up at the stars every night. She told herself that some day she would be living in America, experiencing huge success with a lot of money. She believed it! She prayed to her angels and her guides. She would look at the stars and know there was a way out, even though she didn't know the specifics of this way. The nuns would make fun of her and say, "Oh, you're just dreaming. Why don't you get real and figure out what you're going to do with your life here in this city?" Annie knew that that city wasn't where she was going to be. Twenty-five years later she had the opportunity to move to America and become a citizen. She's now a successful businesswoman who is making a difference by helping children. She helps children learn a trade; she has charity events where they raise money to teach children how to get skills and get into the job market so that they can successfully function in the world. She is living her dream.

Life starts whenever you want it to. You can change your life all the time—every minute, every hour, every day, every week, every month. You have a choice in every move that you make, every breath that you breathe, every thought that you entertain. Imagine if you were to breathe with your full intentional consciousness: each time you inhale, you inhale a breath that enables you to implement your current choice. Imagine that each movement and each thought are charged with the intention of enabling your chosen desires. Imagine the power that all that focused consciousness would generate. This is how you create your life. You are generating that power. It's just that, if you don't bring it into consciousness, it leaks out in all directions. It's still a creative force, but without your intentional consciousness it empowers your unconscious thoughting instead of your intentional thinking. Your task now is to collect and direct that power on to your clearly identified and focused desires—your articulated end results.

The Blockade of Fear

Hesitation and indecision are expressions of fear based on past disappointments and hurts. If we expect the past to repeat itself, it will—*because by expecting it, we have already made a choice!* We are living into that end result. If we fail to focus on the changes we want and fail to invite them into our lives, the status quo will keep on being the status quo; we have chosen that by failing to order something different. It's like going into a restaurant and habitually ordering "the regular" instead of exploring the menu and daily specials. Fear will keep us paralyzed, stagnant. We get stuck by wondering whether we are deserving, or whether our desires are pure. I am here to tell you that if you bring your full consciousness and intentionality—your mindfulness—to your desires, you can absolutely trust them.

Our true desires are themselves an expression of our spirituality. Our spirituality is itself an extension of Universal good. In the Spiritual Zone we can trust that our desires are holy and completely deserving. By identifying and pursuing our desires in a focused, specific, mindful way, we are serving our true spiritual destiny by bringing more love, more good, more happiness and more abundance into the world. This is the whole purpose of our incarnation.

The Choice of Love

I have a client I'll call Dharma, who is more awake than most, and for the most part really lives her life in the Spiritual Zone. She is mindful and intentional in how she maintains her body, her thinking and her emotions. She came to me with a concern that she feels a tremendous attraction for a coworker, Tim. Both Dharma and her coworker are happily married. Nonetheless, Dharma finds herself thinking about Tim, dreaming about him during her sleep life, going out of her way to be in his presence at work. She described that it wasn't particularly a sexual attraction, but that she could imagine channeling the attraction in a sexual way. She found it unusual that she didn't really want anything from Tim, she just wanted to be able to give to him. She sent him loving, positive thoughts. She supported him at work, helping him to do well, and to be successful. She came to me to talk about this because Tim had become such an encompassing interest for her. She wanted to know if this was okay.

In the Spiritual Zone we have tremendous power and capacity relative to the passive, sleepy way we have lived previously. In the Zone we are so awake that we recognize our allies in spirituality. Sometimes they recognize us as well; other times, they haven't yet awakened as fully as we have. We might feel an inclination or even a responsibility to help wake them up—just as I feel a responsibility in this book to help wake you up. In the Spiritual Zone we become so awakened to our capacity for unconditional love that we can't help wanting to help others. Initially, this will extend to our identified loved ones—our spouses, children, parents, siblings, close friends. But as we deepen our commitment to living in the Spiritual Zone, we will find our unconditional love extends outwards to the next circle—our close community of our church, coworkers, neighbors, the fellow families at our child's school.

This is what Dharma is experiencing with her coworker, Tim. She finds herself loving him unconditionally. Her capacity for this love has jumped from the innermost circle of her intimate personal relationships to the next circle, beginning with this particular coworker. I helped her to see that what she feels for him is, simply, love. She doesn't want anything from him; she isn't particularly sexually attracted to him; she is deeply content with her husband. She loves Tim—*because love is our natural response to other beings once we have reached the clarity of the Spiritual Zone.* In the Spiritual Zone Dharma is free to follow her natural inclinations to love this coworker. She is not seeking to be lovers with him; she simply loves him.

Dharma has a choice to let Tim know this or not. Well, let me rephrase that: she has a choice to tell him she loves him or not. On a spiritual level, Tim knows she loves him. She can choose to let her love for him remain on this level. It may sound odd to you at first, but she can choose to love him without it becoming personal. By this, I mean without engaging his personality. She can simply love him and continue to support him because loving is her natural response to him as a fellow spiritual being.

This experience is both thrilling and unsettling for Dharma. It's thrilling because it feels so good to have opened her heart to this fellow being without seeking anything in return. Unconditional love is a tremendous, self-satisfying capacity of human beings living in the Spiritual Zone. It's new to Dharma that she has grown her capacity to love beyond the immediate circle of her personal relationships. It will continue, though, now that she has taken this first step. Dharma will find herself coming to more and more of her human interactions through her unconditional love. As we grow more and more deeply into the Spiritual Zone, we find ourselves reaching out further and further into the concentric circles of our lives in a profoundly loving way.

This is the spiritual impulse of the great saints: traditional saints such as St. Francis of Assisi, who extended his love out into the circle of the animal kingdom, and contemporary saints such as Mother Teresa or Mahatma Gandhi, who expressed their unconditional love far beyond the personal circle to serve huge numbers of fellow beings experiencing all levels of humanity. Each of these examples—Dharma, St. Francis, Mother Teresa and Gandhi—made a choice to be conscious, intentional human beings. By doing so, they have entered into the Spiritual Zone, where the illusion of their separateness from others begins to evaporate, and unconditional love becomes the currency of social interaction.

You, too, have made the choice to be on this path. When you chose this book, you stepped across the threshold into the Spiritual Zone. You have clearly identified your end result. You are in the tremendously supportive company of beings of great capacity. Welcome home.

EXERCISES, PART ONE

This series of exercises is designed to help you become more fully conscious in your life, leading you out of sleepy illusion and into the clarity of the Spiritual Zone. I find it is effective really to meditate on the particular questions—which could become a project of several days. Let the answers percolate up through your psyche; sleep on the questions and see what different responses you find within your deeper self. I find it is also effective to write the answers in a notebook, so you can return and add to them as deeper insights continue to come to you.

1. What are your major blocks in life? Design five ways you can choose to overcome each one.
2. What significant life decisions have you been postponing? Bring them to clarity for yourself.
3. Do you make decisions based on your own inner voice? Do others influence your decisions?
4. What feelings come up when you don't make the right choice or decision? Practice identifying these feelings, and they will serve you as alarm clocks in your life choices.

5. Are you blaming anyone for making a decision for you? Who are they? Please forgive them now.

   I forgive _____ for _____ now.

6. Write down the five happiest moments in your life. Let the feelings associated with these moments become familiar to you.

7. What would get you excited about your life if you were to have it right now?

8. How would you feel if you had it already?

9. Make a detailed list of your talents—everything you think or know about yourself that is special.

10. List all the people that you are still angry with, and holding a negative thought about. Why?

11. What would happen if you forgave all these people and all things in your life?

The truth is if you forgave everything in life you would be set free to be your true divine self.

EXERCISES, PART TWO

Now complete these questions for yourself. Be honest:

1. What is your secret desire to have in this world?
   a. To be?
   b. To do?

2. If money weren't an issue for you, what would you do in life?
   a. Have?
   b. Be?
   c. Buy?

3. My ideal career is _____.

4. My ideal relationship is _____.

5. My ideal body is _____.

AFFIRMATIONS

Speak and write the following affirmation in your journal or notebook. Return to focus on the ones that really resonate for you, and make them a daily practice:

1. I am accepting all miracles in my life—now!
2. I am now lovingly appreciating myself and others.
3. I am trusting myself, my unlimited potential.
4. I am confident, making only the best decisions.
5. I accept only the best in life.
6. I give myself permission to be vulnerable.
7. I am loving and confident.
8. I am trusting my inner voice.
9. I give myself permission to live as I choose.

Think of these affirmations as tools for the journey. Use them to reinforce your intention to be in the Spiritual Zone at every opportunity you have for choice in your life. They will help you to recognize that you always have choice and that every choice you make can propel you toward the Spiritual Zone.

5

Recognizing You Have Support

Modern life often interferes with the close relationships that once characterized the traditional extended family. Loneliness and depression due to isolation are unfortunately common complaints in the Western world. The majority of Western people now live in urban and suburban areas, yet, ironically, this close proximity to others has bred isolation and autonomy rather than close, sustaining relationships. Society is fractionated along so many lines: socioeconomic, racial, political, religious, intellectual. There are categories and subcategories of social groups identified according to specific common interests. Participating in these groups can yield the opportunity for relevant contact with other like-minded people, but often does not give the deep, reassuring sense of belonging that people hunger for in order to satisfy their innate human need for spiritual contact.

You Are Not Alone

As my client from the previous chapter, Dharma, has started to experience, the Spiritual Zone is a miraculous community rich with profound and meaningful opportunities for spiritual relationships. The Zone is your spiritual community. Membership in this community is your royal birthright. As you connect with other Zone denizens as Dharma has begun to do, you will experience that the Spiritual Zone is the loving community that your innermost self has always longed for. You have it now.

The Illusion of Isolation

Prior to awakening into the Spiritual Zone, we lived in an ego-centered world. We habitually judged others as better or worse than ourselves, with the subconscious but intentional result of setting ourselves apart from them. We preferred to think of ourselves as isolated, solitary individuals, and we concocted all kinds of reasons to convince ourselves that we were undeserving of deep contact and spiritual communion with others.

These are the habits of the ego as it struggles for sovereignty over our lives; the ego that fears it will be crushed and abandoned if we surrender our lives to our awakened spirituality. Letting go of a vigilant, determined-to-be-sovereign ego can be difficult; this ongoing challenge is intensified by the heightened consciousness of characterizing all your choices as ones either of love or of fear. The ego is fear-based; the heart is love-based. If you are struggling with ambivalence as you progress through this book, you are experiencing the reactions of your fear-based, self-protective ego not wanting to surrender its sovereignty to your higher, love-based spiritual consciousness. Until now, this ego has functioned as an effective valve, keeping you safe from its perceived dangers—and for this it must be honored. However, it has also deprived you of the gifts of spiritual communion by subscribing to the illusion that you are separate—separate from your spiritual nature and from that of others. For this mistake it must be forgiven.

Outgrowing Ego Sovereignty

As we move forward together into the higher consciousness of the Spiritual Zone, we begin to outgrow the tight confines of the ego. Through the message and practices of this book, we have come to identify with our infinitely expansive spiritual selves—which will neither crush nor abandon the ego, but, rather, lovingly contain it, appreciate it for its appropriate usefulness and forgive its mistaken illusions of sovereignty. In traveling to the Spiritual Zone, we are embarking on a noble and holy quest for love. Fearlessly embracing the truth and readily offering forgiveness are our invincible tools. Full hearts, abundance and a deeply felt loving communion with all of life will be our just rewards.

You are not alone. I am with you. So are millions of others. We treasure you. You are unique and irreplaceable. You are an integral part of the great All That Is. Believe me. It is only the arrogance of the ego that causes you to doubt otherwise—that you are an isolated, separate individual pitted against other isolated, separate individuals competing for limited resources. From the perspective of the Spiritual Zone, this delusion is perfectly unmasked. You and I are no more separate than two apples growing on the same branch. We are each intimately connected through our shared abundant origins in the tree of life.

Your ego thinks its job is to fight others in order to protect its survival. When it feels its own authority is threatened, it will fight with you as well. How do we deal with this? In a word—*forgiveness*. We forgive our egos for not knowing any better. We forgive ourselves for allowing our egos and their agenda of separation to have dominance in our lives. We atone for this mistake. The illusion of separation is healed by atonement, by at-one-ment. Atonement properly aligns our identities as a part of the great All That Is. Atonement is achieved by forgiveness.

The Joy of Atonement

There are not separate ego boundaries in the Spiritual Zone. We all exist together in the Universal flow. Like my client Dharma, you have found or will find yourself impersonally loving individuals in your life. In the Zone, abundant love courses through you, flowing freely into those whom you come in contact with (and also those you only think about and imagine). Once your habitual judgment falls away, you begin to feel a deep connectedness with every human being, indeed with all of life. We are all expressions of life; we are light crystallized into vibrant physical form. We express ourselves as love. What did the Beatles say? "I am he as you are he as you are me and we are all together." Together, we are life!

As you practice mindfulness, you will continue to grow increasingly awake. Your intuition will develop, perhaps even astonishingly at first. This is because you are not separate. You overlap with all life. There are spiritual parts of you that are held in common with others. In these common areas your natural response to others is recognition, sympathy and compassion. You will feel the pain and loneliness of the lost and confused, and your melting heart will expand to include them. In the Spiritual Zone, atonement will be your response to others—you will feel a drive for deep contact. This is unconditional love acting through you. Unconditional love is its own reward: you give it because it feels good and right, regardless of the response.

Fellow Spiritual Travelers

You are not alone in the Spiritual Zone. Trust me. You have millions of wide-awake family members all around you. They hold you in their midst like a delighted grandmother cuddles her infant grandchild for the first time. As you strengthen your comfort and familiarity in the Zone, your home place, you will begin to recognize others. Others are already recognizing you. Don't believe me? Feeling impatient? Carry this book around, make it visible, and see what happens. See who approaches you and what conversations ensue. You are moving in a sea of fellow spiritual travelers. Believe me. I am only one of the many.

In the beginning, you may feel timid about making contact. This is the residue of ego sovereignty, where you once presumed that others were unsafe or uninteresting or disinterested. Traveling on the flow of unconditional love, you are safe. In the Zone, your caring and compassion are so activated and attuned that you will find everyone is interesting. Your compassionate Zone energy is so attractive that no one will be disinterested in you—if they too are awake. If they're not yet awake and you approach them with caring and compassion, you will begin to awaken them. Believe me, everyone is hungry for, and delighted by, the loving energy you have begun to emanate.

In the Zone we recognize our responsibility to awaken others. It is felt as an urgent desire to share. You don't want your loved ones to miss out on the majesty and miracles that have become your life. This is a primary drive of the spiritual human being. We recognize ourselves in all beings. We seek union through love.

As you travel deeper into the Zone, you will feel this desire growing more potent within you. At the same time, you may feel timid; a lifetime spent in fear of pain or rejection may still impact you so that outreach to others feels risky. That's okay. You just need a little practice.

Finding a Traveling Companion

So let's practice. I want you to identify a "spiritual ally" to be your conscious traveling companion in the Zone. This could be your partner/lover, sibling, coworker or a friend. It could be someone who strikes up a conversation after seeing you carrying this book on the subway. This will be someone with whom you can consciously decide to share mutual support. If you don't receive immediate clarity about this person's identity, that's okay. Relax and trust that they are heading toward you. Be ready to give your unconditional support to whoever arrives to travel with you.

Wanting Versus Having

I want to tell you the story of a client who has become a friend of mine, Alex. Alex was in his early thirties and had done a considerable amount of spiritual work before I met him—reading, study, yoga, meditation, affirmations. He was always striving. He hadn't yet met the concept of the Spiritual Zone, but he was nevertheless knocking on the door. He had sought my help because he felt stuck when it came to manifesting the relationship, the primary love relationship, that he wanted for himself. He had been through a series of monogamous love relationships with different women lasting from a couple of months to five years. Usually, he had left the relationships because he felt spiritually dissatisfied. This had been going on for twelve years. Alex expressed that he knew he was meant to have a life partner to marry and have children with, but he was becoming frustrated and disillusioned because it seemed he was having a helluva time finding her.

I agreed with Alex that he would have such a partner. I could see him in this relationship. I helped him to see that the intensity of his desire was interfering with the satisfaction of that desire. All his creative power had been attached to his desire, to the wanting, instead of to the end result, to the having. I was able to reassure Alex that his partner was indeed real, and that she was out there looking for him as well. I encouraged him to trust that she was on her way, and that his perfect confidence in this fact would be the beacon that led her to him. I encouraged him to seek her internally instead of externally, to quiet himself and feel her presence already in his life, to trust that they had made a spiritual agreement to find each other and be together, and that they had made agreements with others who would be their children. I reassured him that he did not need to search randomly and erratically for women who might be the one. The one was on her way to him.

I warned Alex that she might not look like he expects; as we discussed in Chapter Two, our Spiritual Zone partners may not follow in the pattern of those we previously thought were our "type." Our type is no longer designated by our cultural or sexual desires, rather by our unconditionally loving hearts, which love without prejudice or judgment.

Alex did find the woman who has become his wife. They met in a yoga class. He had observed her for a long time in the class, attracted by her radiance. He hadn't considered her as a potential partner because she appeared to be so young—a teen, he thought. When they met "coincidentally" at a party one night, Alex found out that she was in fact twenty-three. He asked her to dinner and trusted his unconditional love to direct the relationship. They soon recognized each other. Alex realized that his twelve-year search had been somewhat ridiculous; he'd started looking for her when his partner was only eleven! The lesson? Trust that relationships have their perfect pace and that miracles have their perfect timing. I'm sharing this story in order to remind you that like attracts like, that there is absolutely the perfect mate for you.

Your Traveling Companion

In our immediate practice in this chapter, there is the perfect spiritual ally to accompany you as you progress into the Spiritual Zone. Right now, in this exercise, you are not looking for a lover or a life partner; you are simply looking for a traveling companion. This is a practice. In this practice, you are learning to trust yourself to make the right relationship and to share experiences for mutual gain.

This relationship with your traveling companion may be temporary, but it is not insignificant. It may be the first intentional, consciously spiritual relationship you have experienced. You may find yourself traveling with someone who on the surface looks like you share nothing in common. Know that that's okay. This relationship isn't about your romantic or social or business or intellectual interests. You are traveling companions. You're both going to the Spiritual Zone. Just like all kinds of people visit Italy for all kinds of reasons, so do all kinds of people travel to the Spiritual Zone. You are attracted to the Zone for all kinds of reasons, but ultimately you will discover that you have come to the Zone to be your true self.

I am encouraging you to find a traveling companion for two reasons: one, to make the trip easier on yourselves, helping each other with directions and baggage when it gets too heavy; and two, to practice being in community, the natural state in the Spiritual Zone, where ego isolation has given way to deep union among spiritual beings. By engaging deeply with a traveling companion, together you will be acting as if you were familiar, long-time Zone residents (which you are).

How are you going to find your traveling companion? You are going to expect them to arrive beside you; you are going to make your needs known by revealing widely and casually that you are reading this book; you are going to respond to all inquiries in a positive, welcoming manner without judgment.

What are you going to do with your traveling companion? You are going to trust and share. Trust that you can be as open to revealing your traveling experiences as you like. Trust that your companion is not making judgments about you. Trust that compassion, caring and impersonal love are the currency of your interactions. Trust that this is the experience of your higher consciousness coming forward into intentional relationship with another. Share yourself freely and honestly. Reveal your feelings and vulnerabilities. Share your concerns and questions about what you experience. Share your fears so that they may be dissolved in the comforting reassurance of unconditional love.

If it feels awkward getting started, read this book together. Approach this relationship as if you had advertised in your newspaper for a traveling companion to Italy. Talk about your expectations, your particular interests and concerns. Just as if you were seeking a traveling companion to Italy, look at this relationship as having a particular purpose and a particular time frame. It doesn't have the pressure of having to please all aspects of your life for an indefinite time. If it helps you to be more comfortable, create some boundaries. For example, decide to meet for two hours a week for two months, and then re-evaluate.

Okay, enough talk. Let's get started. It is time for you deeply to experience in your soul that you are not alone. I'm eager for you to know the bliss of this reality.

EXERCISES

Write answers to the following questions in your journal or notebook where you can return to them to add further insights as you work your way through the mission of this chapter. They will help you to know yourself better, and it is your authentic self who will enter into this temporary traveling companion relationship in the Zone.

1. Write down how you would like to be treated by the people you come into contact with in life.
2. Observe and enumerate the types of friends you would like to have.
3. Make a list of the qualities you would like in a friend.
4. List the names of the people in your life whom you feel are depressed, down and unappreciated.
5. What did you want from them in the first place?
6. List the ideal qualities you would like in your relationships in all areas of your life.
7. What are the ways that you distance yourself from others?
8. List ten ways in which you acknowledge others, love others and inspire others.

9. Share your true feelings. Say, I am feeling _____.
10. What are you holding back?
11. Who is it that you cannot tell the truth to?
12. How will they react if you tell the truth?
13. Ask yourself, where am I unwilling or afraid to seek the truth and speak it?
14. Make a list of every blessing you have.

🍂 AFFIRMATIONS 🍂

Frequently remind yourself verbally and in writing that:

1. I am a loving and gentle person.
2. I have passion and aliveness in all my relationships.
3. I speak only the highest thoughts for everyone and everything.
4. I use my powerful words to inspire magnificence in others.
5. I share and communicate my true feelings with everyone.
6. I only attract people who have my similar vision and support my greatness.
7. All my friendships support my spiritual vision.
8. I am grateful and appreciative for all my blessings.
9. I find the good in every person.
10. I have complete harmony in all my experiences.
11. My life is great!

READER/CUSTOMER CARE SURVEY

We care about your opinions! Please take a moment to fill out our online Reader Survey at **http://survey.hcibooks.com.**
As a **"THANK YOU"** you will receive a **VALUABLE INSTANT COUPON** towards future book purchases as well as a **SPECIAL GIFT** available only online! Or, you may mail this card back to us and we will send you a copy of our exciting catalog with your valuable coupon inside.

(PLEASE PRINT IN ALL CAPS)

First Name _____ MI. _____ Last Name _____

Address _____ Email _____ City _____

State _____ Zip _____

1. Gender
☐ Female   ☐ Male

2. Age
☐ 8 or younger   ☐ 13-16
☐ 9-12   ☐ 21-30
☐ 17-20   ☐ 31+

3. Did you receive this book as a gift?
☐ Yes   ☐ No

4. Annual Household Income
☐ under $25,000
☐ $25,000 - $34,999
☐ $35,000 - $49,999
☐ $50,000 - $74,999
☐ over $75,000

5. What are the ages of the children living in your house?
☐ 0 - 14   ☐ 15+

6. Marital Status
☐ Single
☐ Married
☐ Divorced
☐ Widowed

7. How did you find out about the book?
(please choose one)
☐ Recommendation
☐ Store Display
☐ Online
☐ Catalog/Mailing
☐ Interview/Review

8. Where do you usually buy books?
(please choose one)
☐ Bookstore
☐ Online
☐ Book Club/Mail Order
☐ Price Club (Sam's Club, Costco's, etc.)
☐ Retail Store (Target, Wal-Mart, etc.)

9. What subject do you enjoy reading about the most?
(please choose one)
☐ Parenting/Family
☐ Relationships
☐ Recovery/Addictions
☐ Health/Nutrition
☐ Christianity
☐ Spirituality/Inspiration
☐ Business Self-help
☐ Women's Issues
☐ Sports

10. What attracts you most to a book?
(please choose one)
☐ Title
☐ Cover Design
☐ Author
☐ Content

TAPE IN MIDDLE; DO NOT STAPLE

FOLD HERE

Comments

6

Reprogramming Yourself to Change Old Patterns

Imagine again that you are headed to Rome. Your first-class flight has just taken off and you're perfectly comfortable. Carlo, your dashing Italian flight attendant, has just fluffed your pillow and brought you a Cinzano. You have tucked all your traveling supplies comfortably within reach, making your broad, leather, first-class seat into a cozy nest. You have the pleasant, startling awareness that you are living your fantasy vacation. You have leveled off at cruising altitude and are settling in to get to know your traveling companion sitting beside you. She has a pleasant, inviting demeanor and begins asking you gentle questions about yourself.

You suddenly realize you have a broad choice in your answers. This is your fantasy vacation: you can be whomever you want. Maybe a few days ago you were a deathly bored housewife getting fat on too many chips, or a car salesman with no customers, or an actress who has been waitressing away her prime. Maybe you were a worrier or a depressive or a chronic apologizer who knew her apologies were alienating her husband and her teenage son and most of her old friends, but who nevertheless felt so sorry about herself that she just couldn't help her obsessive apologizing.

You realize none of that matters any longer. You are now sitting in Alitalia first class, and your legs are stretched out and your feet are relaxing on a fold-down footrest in your plush new terrycloth slippers, courtesy of Carlo. Your Cinzano is beginning to taste familiar. You can be whomever you want. Do you answer your seatmate with information about your dreary past—or do you seize this opportunity to create the life that you want right now? You can still be the hard-luck salesman or you can be the international traveler who is pursuing his curiosity about Michelangelo. Both are accurate. The choice is yours.

Who Do You Want to Be?

In the Spiritual Zone we are awakened to the realization that in every instant of our lives we are making a choice. Our whole lives are a creative act. If we're asleep at the wheel of our lives, we are following our own choice to be asleep. The intent and practices of this book have been to wake you up to the recognition that you have a choice at every instant in your life. Moving sleepily through life, we tend to make the same choices instant after instant. Patterns and habits develop, and we mistakenly make believe that we are subject to these patterns and habits, as if we are them. The reality is that we have *chosen* them.

No matter where we are living or how we are living, we are the creators of our own lives. In the Spiritual Zone the critical difference is that we are *conscious* creators of our own lives. We bring mindfulness and intention and right thinking to the thousands of instantaneous choices we make each day. At the end, our day is the composite of all these choices. In our passive pre-Zone sleep state, we weren't really aware of how we got from point A to point B—it felt like something that simply happened to us. We called it luck or fate; we felt fortunate or victimized, depending on the event. Now, in the heightened consciousness of the Spiritual Zone, we recognize this was a delusion of our sleepiness.

We had been living a mistake. Now we are awake to that fact. So do we beat ourselves up for those wasted years? No—we simply forgive ourselves. In the pre-Zone state, we didn't know any better. Now we do. We correct our mistakes and forgive the past. After all, it got us to where we are today.

Mistakes as Learning Tools

It is easy to see the mistakes of others. As parents, we watch our children make mistake after mistake; wise parents recognize that this is how children learn. We let our children make their own mistakes—of course, always providing for their safety. If we intervene before they have a chance to act for themselves, they get the message that we don't trust their ability to choose. They lose confidence in themselves and in their choices. Parents who do this—and many parents do—may be acting in what they believe to be the best interests of their children, but they are making a mistake. Controlling and overprotective parents take choice and self-confidence away from their children at infancy. Their children grow up experiencing confinement, feeling frustrated, angry, deeply confused and separated from their innate freedom to make the choices that create their own lives. They have been separated from their personal power.

A couple came to see me, hoping to get some spiritual insight into their eight-year-old daughter, Cissy, who was having a lot of difficulty at school—socially with other children and in the classroom, and also expressed as continual defiance of her class teacher. The parents were distraught. They explained that they had changed their lives and that the mother had taken time off from her professional career to be truly available to their daughter during her early years. They had sacrificed to place her in the best private school in their area. They volunteered countless hours at the school; between the two of them they did volunteer playground duty every day of the week. They bought only the best of everything for Cissy. They were trying valiantly to be perfect parents.

No doubt this couple's intentions were high and selfless. They were, however, unfortunately mistaken about how to be good parents. Their constant interventions in Cissy's eight-year-old life had preempted Cissy's ability to make her own choices. She couldn't even play with her classmates at recess without their oversight and intervention. The parents thought they were selfless in their parenting; in fact they were dictators. They had eclipsed Cissy's freedom at every opportunity for decision, telling her how to dress, how to behave, whom to play with and even how to play! Cissy felt confined by her parents' choices on her behalf. Her parents' actions didn't feel loving and supportive to her; instead, Cissy felt that they didn't trust her and they didn't believe in her capacity to make correct choices for herself. She was terribly confused.

They told her they loved her, and, like every child, Cissy chose to believe this with every fiber of her being. However, Cissy did not experience her parents' behavior as loving; it was distrusting and it undervalued her worth. The result was that Cissy felt confused and smothered. She needed to rebel against the tight constraints. As an eight-year-old she wasn't going to risk her parents' love, so Cissy chose to rebel against her teacher and her classmates instead.

It is taking a lot of work for Cissy's well-meaning parents to reprogram the complex delusions they have built around their parenting. They had seen themselves as ideal, self-sacrificing parents when in fact they had robbed their daughter of her freedom. The hopeful thing is that they now realize that they made mistakes and they recognize that they have the power to correct them through forgiveness and mindful parenting in every present instant.

I choose to share this story because each of us was somehow stifled by our parents when we were growing up. Some of us were actively abused by unhealthy parents (who were most likely abused themselves), but a much greater percentage of us were caused to suffer by the well-meaning actions of parents who thought they were doing their best. The great majority of them were partially asleep, unaware that they could be making more conscious, immediately relevant choices in every instant of their parenting. More than likely, they had bought into a vague, encompassing picture of what "good parenting" looked like and then surrendered their future parenting choices to this pre-programming.

The human race cannot afford to do this any longer! Unconscious parenting leads to unconscious children, who grow up to be unconscious adults who elect unconscious or manipulative leaders who increase rather than heal world suffering. We must raise our children in the Spiritual Zone, and the only—and certain—way to do this is to ensure that we are living in the Spiritual Zone ourselves. In the heightened consciousness of the Spiritual Zone we can forgive and heal our pasts—and dramatically improve our influences in the world as we go forward into life with mindfulness and intentionality. The more awake we are, the more information we have to make the right conscious choices for ourselves in every moment.

Healing Mistakes to Increase Flow

In Chapter Three we studied forgiveness as the tool to correct our past mistakes and reestablish atonement. Forgiveness is a lifelong practice; because we are imperfect humans we will continue to make mistakes. This is how we learn. As we progress deeper into the Zone, however, we will make fewer and fewer mistakes because of having brought more consciousness to each of our choices along the way. This heightened mindfulness will also enable us to recognize our mistakes sooner so that they become little bumps instead of considerable detours on the journeys of our lives.

The more we are able to recognize our mistakes, and the more consciousness we bring to the multitude of choices that compose our lives, the more we feel throughout our lives that we are living in spiritual flow. We begin to recognize a deeper connectedness to those in our inner circle and an impersonal heart connection to all of life. Our capacities for sympathy, empathy and compassion are enhanced—for ourselves as well as for all of life. We allow ourselves to feel the inherent value that we as individuals bring to all of life; we gradually come to realize and appreciate that no one can do what we do, no one can contribute what we contribute, and no one can love how we love. We are unique manifestations of the Universal Spirit.

Expanding Self-Image

As we expand our pictures of ourselves from challenged, isolated, petty, unconscious individuals to intentional, unique, compassionate spiritual beings within an intentional spiritual Universe, our capacities expand and our self-esteem soars. This is not ego gratification, where we celebrate ourselves in relationship to our judgments over others. Rather, we begin to see ourselves as integral parts of the interconnected whole of life. We feel deeply honored by the opportunity to participate. We recognize that we have come with a precise and unique combination of skills and gifts and experiences to address the destiny of our lives with heartfelt intention. We do not measure ourselves against others; in fact we do not measure ourselves at all. Our powers of discrimination are heightened, but our propensity towards critical judgment dissolves. We are swimming in the flow of consciousness.

This healed image of ourselves brings with it tremendous healing of our self-esteem. Living in the Spiritual Zone, we truly experience ourselves as fountains of the Universal spirit. We feel we have access to tremendous capacities. In this flow, our expanded awareness affords us a deeper intuitive knowing. We become more and more sensitive to others through the feeling realm. The old judgments and self-judgments we held fade into irrelevancy. The profound trust that comes with this deep connectedness satisfies our security needs. Living consciously and intentionally centered in our hearts, we align our sexual drives with authentic expressions of love. We access our amplified personal power to meet our own needs but also for impersonal good works. By forgiving past mistakes and making mindful choices in every instant of our present lives, we find ourselves transformed into powerful, loving, giving beings.

As we grow more and more awake in the Spiritual Zone, we find ourselves changing to align with our new consciousness. Assumptions that we've made about ourselves or our relationships or other aspects of our lives—sometimes very long-held assumptions—may no longer feel appropriate to our newly awakened selves. Just like that polyester suit we threw away in Chapter Two, we find ourselves rejecting outmoded identities and forgoing circumstances and relationships that no longer resonate with our awake, contemporary selves in the Zone.

Ramifications of Change

A man I'll call James came to one of my seminars. He had recently turned fifty, and he had been doing inner work for some time. Celebrating his birthday, James came to the realization that he had very likely lived half of his life already. He regretted that he hadn't lived it fully awake. He had no more use for reticence and for self-consciousness. He felt a sudden urgency to live the remainder of his life as fully awake as he could be and exactly as he wanted. In light of this, James had begun to implement changes in his life, reprogramming himself and his relationships to reflect his present needs and desires. This felt invigorating to him; he was breathing new life into all his activities and commitments. He was a self-employed architect, and in his work he decided that he would only do what he enjoyed and was good at—and delegate the rest.

This caused some upheaval in his firm, but as the dust settled James could see that the reorganization was taking root; he was happier and more effective in his work time and that was beginning to have a positive effect on his staff and clients. He experienced that his newfound clarity brought him clients who were also themselves more clear. His work became more satisfying and more interesting. I pointed out to him that this is the experience of living in the flow of the Spiritual Zone: where, before, our confusion attracted confusion, in the Zone our clarity attracts clarity. As the lone proprietor at the top of his small firm, James used to feel isolated in his work. Now he was beginning to feel a general connectedness to others—employees, colleagues and clients alike. James now saw them all as a team working on behalf of a common vision. His relations with others deepened; he found he cared more about their lives and interests and concerns. He had begun relating to them as fellow human beings in the Zone instead of as staff draftsmen.

Full of confidence about the changes he made in his business, James also began to reprogram his family relationships in order to update those old patterns to fit his awakened vision of his life better. Confident that he was bringing more truth and clarity and goodness into his family dynamic, James moved eagerly forward, expecting his wife and two teenage sons to jump on board simply because he knew it was right. This is where James ran into trouble. He was acting on his early experience of the Spiritual Zone without having truly awakened to and developed the necessary compassion to deal responsibly with all the human repercussions of his actions. In fact, James was only half awake. The unilateral actions that had been so effective in his sole-proprietorship business wreaked havoc on the community of his family. His wife felt insecure, fearing that she would be abandoned in her husband's newfound zeal for recreating his life. His sons, having always lived in a stable and relatively predictable family environment, were confused by the sudden changes their father was bringing into their lives.

In working with James, I helped him to understand that responsibility goes along with the sweeping changes he was intent on bringing into his life. He has to awaken all the capacities that will help him successfully to manifest the new vision he has for his life. Chief among these at the moment is the need for the deepening compassion that will enable him to feel with real consciousness his effect upon others, particularly his wife and sons.

As we reprogram ourselves to alignment with the Spiritual Zone, it is critical to bring our heightened awareness of the impact we have in our lives. To understand the way James interconnects with his wife and sons, consider a three-dimensional jigsaw puzzle. Each person connects to each other person in a myriad of ways, and each connection between two of the family members affects the other two members. As James begins to reprogram his life, the parts of himself that protrude into the lives of his family members change shape, some increasing in size, others disappearing, new parts of James sprouting forward.

James had taken for granted how he interfaced with his immediate family. Every internal change upset the external status quo—something James had not anticipated. His wife was suddenly afraid that James's re-evaluation of his life would leave no place for her. His sons, as teenage boys, just wanted to know what they could expect from their dad.

A New Equilibrium

The havoc that James's awakening caused was almost enough to send him back to the old equilibrium. He felt the pain that his changes had brought about in his wife and his boys—and he wanted to undo that pain. This is the point when we came in contact. I coached James that he must be true to his own awakening self. He must trust that being true to himself would only be good for his family. Now, good isn't the same thing as easy. We have all at times become so familiar with our dysfunction that healing it seems a lot more painful than retaining it. However, once we are awake to the recognition of the dysfunction, we must heal it. We have no choice. To our heightened consciousness it will feel inappropriate and not authentically of ourselves, and eventually more painful to retain than to change. We all address necessary changes at our own pace, but once we have identified changes as necessary they must be addressed in order for us to experience our lives in balance.

Changing old patterns takes courage. This is what James realized. He was going to have to dare to upset the status quo of his family in order to be true to himself. This is not a bad thing! This is the Spiritual Zone working through us, flowing from us into our loved ones at those points of our puzzle pieces where we interconnect with them. In his increased capacities, James realized he had to move forward, but he could do so with a new level of love and compassion for the difficulties he was initiating upon his family.

When we enter the Spiritual Zone, we awaken to the realization that we can have anything we want in our lives. We *know* we deserve it. We have a responsibility to ourselves to live our truth, to forgive mistakes we may have made in the past and to reprogram ourselves to change our old patterns. This will likely have ramifications that ripple throughout our lives, into our families and friends and colleagues and work environments. This is all okay. We must simply extend the expanded compassion that accompanies our heightened consciousness to all those who share our lives. We will establish a new equilibrium at a higher, more conscious level within the Spiritual Zone; by reprogramming ourselves we will have uplifted those who share our lives as well. As we learned through James's story, this isn't often easy for others involved. By changing ourselves, we are shaking the familiar constructs of the status quo that we represent in other people's lives. This is our opportunity to speak our truth with love and compassion, and to introduce others to the wondrous changes that the Spiritual Zone offers all of us.

EXERCISES

Contemplate the following questions and answer them in a journal or notebook. They will assist you in the process of letting go of old patterns and reprogramming your life.

1. Notice those times when you are not willing to take a risk. How do you feel?
2. What's involved in the risk?
3. What do you think you will lose?
4. What do you think you will gain?
5. Do you feel guilty when you have taken a risk?
6. Are you afraid you will lose something if you take a risk?
7. What are you afraid of losing?
8. Do you trust yourself with the responsibility for your life?
9. Can you make the right choices in your life?
10. What are those choices?
11. Do you depend on and trust yourself?
12. Do you feel a part of yourself is missing?
13. What is missing in yourself?
14. Examine all failures that you believe you have had. Write down what they are. What do they mean to you?
15. Now forgive all those failures.
16. Write: I forgive myself.
17. Say out loud: I forgive myself.

🍂 AFFIRMATIONS 🍂

Frequently remind yourself verbally and in writing that:

1. I now trust my feelings.
2. I use my intuition for perfect guidance.
3. I expand my comfort zone daily.
4. I am fearless about life.
5. I have self-worth in my life.
6. I trust myself and all others.
7. I trust all my outer riches.
8. I love myself.
9. I let go with peace and love.
10. I allow all others to love and support me.

Part Three

How to Manifest in the Spiritual Zone

7

Getting to Know Yourself
as a Creator

In the previous six chapters we have explored how to get to the
Spiritual Zone and how to stay in the Spiritual Zone once you get
there. Now that you are here to stay, what do you want to manifest for
yourself and for the world? Do you want a new job? Romance? A life
partner? Prosperity? Unlimited wealth? World peace? An end to world
hunger?

Living in the Spiritual Zone, you are consciously connected to the
Universal source. You have learned that thought is creative. You are
learning to be conscious of the choices you make in every instant of your
life. Your compassion, empathy and sympathy for all living things are
developing. You are becoming a fully functioning citizen of the Spiritual
Zone. Now it is time for you to use the Zone resources available to you
to create the life that you want.

What do you want to create for yourself in the Spiritual Zone? Think
of today—and every day—as the first day of your new life. Bring your
mindfulness to exactly where you are as a starting point and determine
your end result, that place where you choose to be. Be specific.
Remember, when you go to a restaurant, you don't simply say, "Feed
me." No, you order a tuna sandwich on wheat bread with lettuce, tomato
and no pickle. If they bring you a grilled cheese, you send it back, right?
You have to maintain your intention on what it is you have ordered.
Some people might decide, "Well, a grilled cheese will be okay; I don't
want to upset the waiter. I guess I'll just eat it." This is a traitorous mistake in life! You must adhere to your commitment to your end result;
otherwise you will drift directionless through life without ever achieving

the satisfaction of creating what you want for yourself.

As human beings, we are inherently creators. Look around our world at what we have created: for better or for worse, everywhere around us is the tremendous impact of our creativity. In our mindfulness we create beautiful art and architecture: look at that Caravaggio; look at the dome of St. Peter's. We also create pollution, poverty, war, disease and suffering. These are the effects of no mindfulness, creations that happen outside the Spiritual Zone. You will recognize that your life is impacted by all kinds of these thoughtless creations, many of which you have created yourself before you awakened your consciousness. Notice them. Notice the possible mess in your checkbook and in your financial life. Notice how you may have settled for an unsatisfying job. Notice that your body may be overweight or weak or addicted or tired all the time. Notice if you are lonely or sexually dissatisfied. Acknowledge—with a huge allotment of forgiveness—that these are all things you unconsciously created for yourself.

Now let's change them. Human beings are inherently creative. We are physical manifestations of the Universal source, incarnated here on planet Earth to experience physical reality and to manifest on the physical plane. You made a contract with yourself to come here and participate fully in creation. Now you have awakened to the reality that you have a choice in every instant of your life; your choice is whether to create intentionally out of a mindful consciousness, or to create unconsciously out of sleepy habits or old indoctrination.

One Step at a Time

You are a fountain of Universal energy, and you can send the flow in any direction you so choose. So what are you going to choose for yourself? The first step is to prioritize your goals. Be specific! How many times have you thought, I'm going to write that book, or I'm going to lose weight, or I'm going to start a new business, or get more clients or establish perfect health or improve my relationships? These are all noble goals to aim for, but somehow you may have got sidetracked along the way. If you had decided to drive to Rome, you wouldn't just get in the car and start driving, would you? No—you would consult a map, plan several stops along the way. You would always be aiming for Rome, but you would take the trip one segment at a time. The short steps that lead to your end result are critical for keeping you on track. Otherwise, you can too easily make a wrong turn, get totally distracted, and forget where you were headed in the first place. So you must be crystal clear on your end result, and equally clear on the sequential steps you are going to take to get there.

Do you want perfect health? Then you must say to yourself, "I AM perfect health." By identifying yourself with your end result, you are not distracted by the "wanting" that has the effect of separating you from your end result. Picture what "I want perfect health" looks like: you are here and perfect health is way over there and there is a sea of distraction between you. When you say, "I AM perfect health," there is no separation. The energy of perfect health is immediately with you and creating perfect health within your body right now. In this way the source is with you. Separation from the source is an illusion that we no longer give credence to in the Spiritual Zone.

So you have established "I AM perfect health" as your end result. Now look at your map. Are you doing everything in your power to create perfect health? Is each health-impacting action you take aligned with your desired end result? Are you spending your time in the company of supportive, healthy people? Are you exercising? Meditating? Are you eating living, sustaining foods? Are you avoiding dead, processed foods? Are you eating consciously to maintain perfect health? (This would preclude eating for emotional comfort, a common, unconscious habit that is a wrong turn for so many who are struggling with their health.) You must keep your eyes on the prize of your end result, and mindfully consider every little step along the way to make certain that you are on target.

Be Specific

The more specific you are in establishing your end result, the sooner it will become manifest in your life. So often in my seminars, I ask people what they want to create. A common example is, "I want to create a new business." Too general! That's like saying you want to go to Italy for a vacation. You can't buy an airline ticket to Italy! You have to be specific: do you want to fly to Rome or Milan or Venice? I coach the person wanting to create a new business to get very specific: "I have a worldwide company that creates popular women's sportswear now," or, "I have a fabulously successful art gallery in SoHo, Manhattan, now."

Be Perfectly Clear

When I work with people to help them formulate and clarify their end results, I notice they frequently allow themselves to get sidetracked by fear and doubt: "I know I want the gallery, but where am I going to get the money?" This question is off task. *The money will come when you get clear on your end result.* The Universe always supports your intentions, whether you are clear or not: when you are clear about your end result, it is clearly delivered to you; if you are vague or confused, vague confusion is what you will create. Picture that your end result is perfectly clear and articulated; your intention creates a pipeline of energy between you, as the creator, and your end result. The energy is supplied by the Universal source, which is always standing by, waiting for our directions about where to supply energy.

What, Not How

When we engage with the "how" of creation instead of the "what" we interfere with the Universal flow. We have compared ourselves to royalty, in that, as children of the Universe, we are entitled to all its precious gifts and resources. We need to learn to consider ourselves deserving of our desires as would a member of the royal family. A king doesn't concern himself with the how of getting things done; he simply gives his command and expects it to be executed. This is the most effective way for us to achieve the results we want. By micromanaging the how, we preclude an infinite number of unknown opportunities from coming into play.

I have a client named Jackson. Jackson was a high-end real estate salesman, but there was no flow to his business. He came to me because he was frustrated that he wasn't having success attracting clients or closing any deals. I asked him if he enjoyed his work, and he said he did not. So I asked him what he would want to do if he could do any job in the world. Jackson said he would like to work in sports, that he was fascinated by all sports and that he knew a lot about the subject. I coached him to be more specific: did he want to play sports? Did he want to manage a sports team? Did he want to be a sports writer? It didn't take much thinking for Jackson to tell me that he would like to work covering sports on television. Just talking about the fantasy, Jackson's energy changed dramatically; the real estate agent who had come into my office was tired and lifeless, but this man talking about his sports career was full of energy and enthusiasm.

I taught Jackson about identifying his end result, and about acting as if I gave him a specific challenge: if he had a job interview with one of the big sports television networks at the end of the week, what would he do to prepare? He told me that hockey was his weak link, and that he would start by reading up on the LA Kings. I encouraged him to do that and to keep his focus on his end result and trust that the Universe would make the bridge from where he was to where he intended to be.

Jackson left my office and drove directly to one of the big bookstores. He asked the clerk if they had any books about the LA Kings. She led him to the correct shelf and the two of them got into a conversation about hockey and sports in general. Jackson was jazzed by the prospect of his new career, and his enthusiasm really shone through in this casual conversation. After a few minutes, a woman came up to him from the shelves across the way. She told Jackson that she couldn't help overhearing their conversation. She told him that her husband worked for a sports network and she would like to introduce them. She gave Jackson her card.

Jackson called me later that afternoon to tell me that he had an interview scheduled with the man. I coached him to continue to act as if— act as if he already had the job because he needed to bring that kind of confidence into the interview. He decided to imagine that he was working for an East Coast network so that he could bring the energy of experience and success into his interview. He hit it off immediately with the executive; they talked sports—Jackson's favorite thing to do—the whole time, and at the end, the man offered Jackson a job. Jackson was incredulous and ecstatic. Now, it may not always happen as quickly as it did for Jackson—but if you are committed to your end result, if you consciously take all the steps along the way that lead to that end result, keeping your focus on what you want and letting the Universe figure out the how, you will absolutely create what you want in life.

Focus Your Power

You are tremendously powerful. You must be careful that you don't give your power over to fears and doubts. When you do this, your tremendous power fuels all the negative things you are giving attention to through your worry and concern. Universal energy is value-neutral. It might help to think of this energy as fuel. It flows where you direct it. It can flow just as readily into your end result of the fabulously successful SoHo gallery as it can into the belief construct that you don't have enough money to make the gallery happen. If this is hard for you to believe, that is simply because you are still new to the Spiritual Zone. The more you live here and trust that you are a fully participating, important, unique creator whose job it is to direct the flow of Universal energy, the more successful experiences you will have to build your new perspective on reality.

It is vitally important that you trust yourself and your desires. You are a creative spiritual being incarnated here on Earth right now to experience manifesting in physical reality. If you can't believe this yet about yourself, believe me—I know this about you. All your mindful, conscious desires are trustworthy. The things you are drawn to have and to create are aligned with the Universal source; it is your particular mission to manifest them here on Earth now. If you are finding yourself in fear or doubt, if you feel that you are manifesting negativity—financial problems, poor health, dissatisfaction in your relationships—recognize that you need to tune back into the Universal source. The Universe always gives you what you need. If you trust this 5 percent of the time, you'll see 5 percent results. If you trust it 100 percent then you will get 100 percent results.

I have a joke for you: A woman was having a frightful nightmare where she was being chased by a terrifying monster. It was big and green-skinned and hairy, slimy and loud. It was gaining on her as she raced through her house looking for a place to hide. Finally it succeeded in cornering her in her living room. As it hovered before her, snorting and drooling, she cried in panic, "What are you going to do to me now?" The monster answered, "How should I know, lady? It's your dream."

All our life is our own creation. We came into this life high and pure, but along the way we bought into the negativity of someone saying we weren't smart enough or pretty enough or capable enough, that we didn't do the right thing or go to the right schools. All these little voices aggregate to become a monster that chases us around the house chattering into our ears. Now is the time to decide that we have a choice whether or not to listen to this chatter, to take responsibility for having created the chatter in our lives. If we choose to validate the chatter, then we are choosing drama over clarity. The drama of "I can't" keeps you from moving to your higher levels. If you need drama in your life, watch soap operas. Your life itself is too valuable to waste on pettiness.

Keep Motivated!

Set up a check-in with your traveling companions. Share your targeted end results with them and ask them to reinforce your end results and to let you know when they sense that you have stepped off track. In the Spiritual Zone we all support each other. In the Spiritual Zone we recognize and acknowledge our oneness. As an expression of your self-love, ensure that you are surrounding yourself with supportive people. Know that you are unlimited and that others are equally unlimited. Support them in this way as they support you.

Do you have lifelong wishes that have yet to be fulfilled? Don't lose sight of them. You can become these wishes by simply trusting that they are good and that you have the power to manifest them here and now.

Tune in to your power as a fountain of the Universal source. As you give yourself permission to live, love, forgive and be in the truth of who you are, you will begin to see transformation within yourself. Your awareness shifts so that you begin to experience the power of success in every instant. Your old patterns will fade until they don't come up any more. You must honor that you bring a unique gift. The more you breathe into this truth, the more you will enable the shift in your consciousness that will manifest your targeted end result.

Speaking Your Intention

The alignment of body, mind and spirit accelerates transformation. The body responds to repetition and practice. When I was a competitive swimmer training for the Olympics, I used to practice two and a half hours every morning and another two and a half hours every afternoon. I built the memory of each perfect stroke into the cells of my body. Now when I get into a pool—even if it has been a year—my body still knows exactly what to do to execute the perfect stroke. We must exercise our will as we initiate change into our lives. The more we reinforce our intention through repetition, the more solid a foundation we are creating. It takes twenty-one days to shift your energy and self-awareness completely. A focused twenty-one days of practicing the affirmations I have shared with you throughout this book will reprogram your body and your expectations. Twenty-one days of clarity and mindfulness focused on your end result will bring it readily into your life. Remember to be very clear in how you frame your end result. Don't say, "I want," or "I need," or "Oh, please." Instead, say, "I AM":

1. "I AM love and I only attract the perfect, loving partner for me right now."
2. "I AM experiencing miracles in all aspects of my life right now."
3. "I AM the proprietor of the hottest art gallery right now."
4. "I AM creativity, and I succeed in all my work endeavors with creative insight, planning and solutions."

Affirmations work because language is powerfully creative. You must bring your conscious into the very words that you use. You know one of the most powerful affirmations I hear all the time? "I'm broke." These two potent words cut off the supply. Energy streaming through a broken pipeline never makes it to the end result. Never say, "I'm broke." It separates you from your unlimited greatness. Keep the power for yourself and try, instead, "I choose not to purchase that right now." Remember that you are royalty, and the royal family gets everything they want. The queen doesn't choose to buy everything that is available to her, and you can make the same choice: "I choose not to purchase that right now."

As you work your way through this handbook, you have probably begun to notice that my intention—my end result for you with this book—is to get you to bring as much mindfulness as you can to every instant of your life. With the practice of this higher consciousness, you will become more fully attuned to your end result, and all your once random actions and words will now have meaning and purpose in helping to create the life that you want. You state your intention, keep focused, and trust that the Universe will provide the means.

You may initially experience this success as magical or miraculous—and then over time you will become accustomed to this reality as the way life is intended. In the States there's a popular bumper sticker that says: "Expect a Miracle." Now is the time to take that quite seriously.

EXERCISES

The following exercises will help you to bring clarity to why you are creating the life you have and how you can create the life that you want. Contemplate the following questions and write your answers in a journal or notebook. Come back and fill in details as they continue to occur to you. By bringing your consciousness to your power over these things, you can change them as you wish.

1. List ten ways that you block yourself from being, doing and having exactly what you want.
2. Practice taking responsibility for what you have in your life right

now. List several things you are pleased you have and also several you would be pleased to be rid of.

3. If you feel that you don't have enough of something—make a list. What is that something or things that you lack? After you have made your list, fill in the blanks:
   a. I create _____ for myself. Now!
   b. I create _____ for myself. Now!
   c. I create _____ for myself. Now!
   d. I create _____ for myself. Now!

4. How do you feel around people who are very wealthy? What is separating you from them?

5. When you are around anyone or anything that you want, your words should be: Isn't it great they have that ? That's for me, too.

6. Whatever you want—see it, say it and be it. Remember your subconscious mind will manifest it somewhere in your life. List ten things you want, using the following declarative forms:
   I am _____. I have _____.

7. Do you blame yourself for your situations? What are they?

8. Let's create your life, the way you want it. Write down and visualize the kind of abundance you would like for yourself. What kind of job would you like? What type of partner/relationship would you like? Where and how would you like to live?

9. What does your house look like? The one you really want? Provide a detailed description as if you were writing to an estate agent you really trust to find this house for you.

10. I want you to write a story book—the story of you. Imagine it is a children's book about you. Let's start: once upon a time (add your name) . . . Now finish your perfect story.

❧ AFFIRMATIONS ❧

Write and speak the following affirmations repeatedly to reprogram your identity as the creator of your own life:

1. I create an abundant Universe, and I accept that abundance now!
2. I always create the perfect opportunities in my life.
3. I enjoy giving money.
4. The more I give, the more I receive.
5. I am a winner!
6. I am already a worldwide success.
7. I am confident.
8. I have a perfect, healthy body.
9. I forgive myself for judging my body or comparing it to another's.
10. The energy of my body empowers me to enjoy a magnificent life.
11. I attract only loving romantic partners into my life.
12. I have unlimited miracles in my life now!
13. I am thankful for my life.
14. I am a magnificent being.

8

Enjoying Spiritual Financial Freedom

It's time to get practical. A large part of manifesting in our Western culture is about money—about having the resources to acquire the physical aspects of the life that you want. Having worked through the previous chapters, you now have a solid foundation and context for developing your capacities to enjoy financial freedom. We will now look at ways to attract money as a means of developing the outer life that you want to manifest.

Living in the Spiritual Zone, we are connected to all living beings. We are connected to nature and to the earth itself as a conscious, living being. We are connected to the Universal source. We are connected to love, prosperity and abundance, and to the flow of Universal energy. Let's keep this in mind as we consider money.

Money as a Lens into Your Life

In this chapter, money will provide you a great service. As a result of its imperial status in our materialistic consumer culture, money is a powerful lens through which we can look at our lives, our values and our view of ourselves. If you are willing to bring mindful consideration to your relationship with money, you will have the opportunity for great personal insight. Getting to clarity about how we feel about money can be an effective magnifier for how we feel about ourselves. As we progress through this chapter, I encourage you to breathe, walk, meditate—do whatever you need to do to take care of yourself and keep yourself centered in the calm, trusting flow of energy that is the Spiritual

Zone. Here you are safe, safe from judgment, from fear and from worry. It is my intention to help you to deconstruct the charged myths about money that you may have adopted for yourself and to remind you that your true home is here in the loving flow of abundance that is the Spiritual Zone.

Money as a Value-Neutral Trading Tool

Believe it or not, money itself is value-neutral. It is simply a convenient, agreed-upon form of energy exchange. I think it will be helpful if we take some time to consider that money has its roots in simple convenience as a means of trading goods and services.

My neighbor, Marianne, grows tomatoes every summer. I have a fig tree in my yard, and Marianne's husband loves figs. All summer long, we trade figs for tomatoes. I couldn't begin to eat all my figs, nor could she eat all her tomatoes; we share the abundance of our gardening energy, and both are richer for the trade.

I trade my friend, Lisa, personal consultations in exchange for typing my manuscripts. My attorney friend, Martin, used to do legal work for immigrant farm workers in exchange for a lug of strawberries. My friend Hank, who owns a comedy club, gives free admissions to his dry cleaner in exchange for free laundry service. Maybe you are a good mechanic and your next-door neighbor loves to be with children; you tune up her car while she takes your child to the park.

All these are examples of friendly, convenient, mutually beneficial exchanges. We all benefit from cooperation; sharing is an inherent aspect of the abundance of the Spiritual Zone—because there is so much to share!

Money is simply a mutually agreed upon convenient means of exchanging and storing energy. Lisa may want a consultation with me at a time when I'm not yet ready for her to type my manuscript. As friends, we can agree to remember "accounts receivable" that we have with each other. In the broader picture of our lives filled with anonymous exchanges of energy, we rely on currency to hold the energy of our accounts. Money enables me to trade my energy through any number of third parties without even knowing the individuals whose energy I am ultimately consuming. All participants in a money system have made an agreement to cooperate for shared convenience. The currency itself— pounds, euros, dollars, pesos, yen—is simply a symbolic storehouse for our energy. The value-neutral currency simply facilitates our agreement to exchange.

Flow

While currency is value-neutral, the energy that currency represents is not value-neutral; it represents our smart thinking and creativity and hard work—our extension of our creator-selves into physical reality. When we are doing what we love, what we are called to do through our intentional, conscious desires, we find ourselves experiencing flow. This flow sometimes feels miraculous as it extends into all aspects of our lives, including our work lives—that part of our lives where we are intentionally making a contribution as creative beings. By our mindful, conscious work, we are intentionally contributing to the flow of Universal energy. The more we output valuable contribution, the more it returns the flow to us. The Universal energy can come back to us as love, as synchronicity, as goodwill, as support for our physical needs; and it can come to us as currency. Currency expands the creative process by enabling us consciously to choose how to return the energy that has been held in the currency back into the flow. How much consciousness we use in the reconverting of currency (also known as spending, investing, gifting) determines how much the currency that has passed through our hands contributes to the Universal flow.

Currency flows to us in direct response to our intentions. It flows freely toward us in correlation to our conscious creativity and to our selfless giving. When we are feeding the flow, it in turn feeds us. So why do so many of us experience issues of lack around money? I believe it is because we have seen it as separate from ourselves. We have separated it from its original purpose, which was to be a placeholder for our energy. I suspect that every one of you reading this book believes that you have significant energy and creative thought to contribute to the flow of Universal energy.

I believe you can simplify complex money issues by practicing a conscious regard for currency as an agreed-upon placeholder for the energy that you know you have in abundance. You already have a comfortable, familiar relationship to the energy you put out into the world; it is an expression of your creative flow. By evolving your thinking about money to see it as a representation of this energy, money becomes something personal, spiritual and alive. You have unlimited access to it because it originates from you, from the results of your energetic output. In the Spiritual Zone, you will become increasingly more conscious and mindful of your output, of everything that you are flowing out into the world. You can rightfully expect that what you contribute to the flow will return to you—and in this culture some of that return will be in the form of money. Expect it as your royal birthright.

Non-Currency Rewards of Flow

It has been my experience in the Spiritual Zone that abundance and prosperity come to me in many ways in addition to currency. I receive direct compensation for my contributions in many diverse ways—like the barter of typing for consultation; I also receive all kinds of "miraculous" manifestations—like meeting my literary agent at exactly the right time from a "random" airline seat-mate or "finding" a hundred dollar bill on the pavement outside the copy store when I had forgotten my wallet. These everyday miracles are exactly what you can expect when you are living in the conscious flow of the Spiritual Zone.

In our (non-spiritual) culture, we have allowed money to be the value of our self-worth. We are judging and being judged for the car we drive, the home we own, the vacations we take, the clothes we wear, the schools our children go to, the clubs we belong to, the stock portfolios and bank accounts we possess. These things have a status value only according to parameters outside the Spiritual Zone. In this outside place, there is no accounting for the everyday miracles that sustain us and enrich our lives. If we lapse in our mindfulness, we can too easily get sucked into this game. "How much are you worth?" becomes a question that we take seriously—as if we could ever truly quantify our "net worth." *All we can quantify is how much currency we have taken out of the flow at any given moment in time.*

What Really Matters

As ridiculous as this is from the Zone perspective, I do appreciate that there is a tremendous cultural pressure to be materialistic and to judge ourselves and others in terms of accumulated possessions. These constant evaluations are continually hurled at us by the advertising media and can take their toll unless we are vigilant in our consciousness about what really matters. I was recently leading a seminar in Toronto, where I asked about 150 people, "How many of you think you are great in life?" How many hands do you think were raised? Five. Five! Only about 3 percent of the room had given themselves permission to live in their greatness. I had people stand up and say, "I am Carol and I am great," or "I am Evan and I am great." This was terribly difficult for these people to do because they had been so programmed to measure their greatness in terms of wealth or fame.

You *are* great, innately great. You are royalty. You are a unique physical manifestation of Universal creative energy that incarnated on Earth to experience physical reality. You are a wonderful, high, spiritual being who only deserves the best. Believe this, and only the best will come to you.

Respecting Money for What It Represents

How you treat your money is significant now that you realize it is a placeholder for your energy. It is important that you respect your money as you respect the hard work that it represents. Your money is an extension of you, so treat it with the respect that you would show yourself. Take time to make it orderly in your wallet or purse. Be mindful of how you handle it so that you bring mindfulness to what it can do for you.

Let's get really clear about your financial issues so that you can identify and correct any blocks that may be standing between you and the great abundant life that you deserve. Give yourself ample time to do the following exercises, but keep with them, moving forward through them at a responsible, consistent pace.

The Four Steps to Financial Freedom

1. Take responsibility

Let's bring some consciousness to the financial situation you have currently created for yourself so that you can make any changes you want.

A. Write down your hopes and fears about money. Don't hesitate—just let your pen flow.

B. Write down your good and bad thoughts about money. Again, don't be self-critical in this process; the faster you write, the more opportunity your unconscious mind will have to add input.

C. Open your awareness to how you speak about money. Pay close attention to how you verbalize financial issues for the next week. Make notes for yourself.

2. Clarify the financial needs of your lifestyle

By calculating exactly what it is you need, you will more easily identify a financial end result that will bring you the comfortable life you desire.

A. Calculate how much it costs you to live the way you like. Itemize your exact financial needs, including shelter, food, clothing, credit cards, debt service, loans, vacation, car, entertainment, and so on.

B. Let's pretend you're an accountant. Construct a balance sheet that lists all your financial assets and financial liabilities.

These exercises may be emotionally difficult for you. You may have gone a long time without looking at your total debt or your accumulated credit card balances. I am coaching you now to move past this fear-based denial. You are going to get very real with

yourself about where you stand; and then you are going to decide
if you are comfortable and satisfied with this place or whether you
would like to make some changes. Breathe. Be courageous.
Proceed. Let's move on to higher ground:

3. **Clean up the mess**

Only you know what your particular mess is. Face it. Approach it
one step at a time. You are going to dismantle systematically the
dysfunction you have created around money in your life—one step
at a time.

   Just as in Chapter One we considered eating for the wrong reasons (comfort, love), so you might be spending for the wrong reasons. I have a client who was a "shop till you drop" gal. She had an
average salaried job as a secretary, but she spent like a superstar
making millions of dollars. Her particular weakness was clothes—
she didn't even wear them, but she just kept buying. Within a year,
she found herself in real trouble. I went to her house and made her
take everything out of her drawers and closets. I kept a running
tally of the costs of what she had spent in the last year. What she
had spent on clothes she doesn't wear was enough to buy a brand-
new car! I got her to cut up her five credit cards right then and
there. We started her working on paying off the lowest card. She
did these Four Steps to Financial Freedom exercises, and really
raised her consciousness around money. She admitted to herself
that she had used spending as a surrogate for loving herself. She
started really loving herself. She learned to respect herself, and to
respect money. Now, six months later, she has managed to pay off
two of her credit cards. She has a new passion—painting. She is
designing a line of greeting cards. She has begun to accept her
greatness and own her power. She is working out, looking younger
and dating men who respect her. Now, your turn:

A. Explore new ways of increasing your income in order to keep
   the inflow higher than the outflow.
B. Study your credit card balances. If they are beyond your
   capacity to pay off within your monthly income, get rid of the

cards—cut them up, or stash them away. Continuing to carry them with you may be an unavoidable temptation.

C. Plan a strategy to pay off your existing balances; brainstorm with your Zone traveling companion or an accountant, so that you get help in your decision about how best to do this.

4. Find the ideal financial planning system that works for you

A. Set your goals for six months; for one year; for two years. It is important to be open to generating more income as you move forward. What is the current amount of money you make? Do you want to double it? Triple it? You are the money magnet. Do things that you love doing. The money flows as long as you consciously participate fully in the flow of spiritual energy. Be careful to stay in the Spiritual Zone and not to shut down from fear or being overwhelmed. If you do shut down, forgive yourself and start over.

B. Identify your financial end results.
   • Do you want to own a house?
   • Do you want a savings account? How much? $50,000? $100,000? A million?
   • Do you want a retirement account?
   • Are you contributing to a charity or worthy cause with your money?
   • Are you telling yourself the truth about what you want financially?

Consider reframing how you look at money situations:

Old Belief System	New Belief System
How come they can have that?	Isn't it great they have everything in life? That's just what I want. That is for me.

Old Belief System	New Belief System
I don't know how I can. Where will the money come from?	I always have so many opportunities to receive money. Money comes easily to me.
It's impossible for me to buy that!	I choose to buy anything at any time.

Gifting

Let's talk about giving money away. In many of the world's religions there is a long tradition of tithing—giving one-tenth of one's income back to the source. This is a profound mindfulness exercise—to reaffirm our belonging to the one source and consciously to contribute to the flow of Universal energy. Giving away part of your income reinforces your belief in an infinite abundance. You are trusting that this tithed amount will go out into the world and support good works and then come back to you. Inherent in this action is your belief that any good works done benefit you personally—because they benefit someone. By tithing, you are practicing your belief in connectedness.

Do not give out of sympathy or pity; these are reinforcing of lack. If you regard someone in chronic financial need, give them your love, give them this book; simply giving them money can reinforce the status quo circumstances of dependency that are clearly not working for them.

Just as I have encouraged you to trust and follow your conscious desires about what to do with your life, so can you trust your conscious desires about what and whom to support with your financial gifts. By giving to enable the good works of others, you will quickly experience the power of your money to do good in the world. This reinforces your own sense of deserving more—which will lead to your having more.

I have some friends, Larry and Belinda, who have practiced tithing for several years. They devised a system that is very effective, and I would like to share it with you. First, they opened a new current account. On the account name, and just below their names on the upper left-hand corner of the checks, they had printed "Tithe Account." Then, whenever they received any income—pay checks, interest, dividends, financial gifts—they immediately deposited one-tenth of their own income into the tithe account. They let the money in this account accumulate for three months, so that it represented a considerable amount. They did some research about worthy causes and decided that they wanted to give to four different causes: in their case, the ashram where they did their spiritual practice, the environment, supporting people with AIDS, and education.

As the "give-away" money in their tithe account grew over three months, Larry and Belinda began to feel truly wealthy. They found themselves reading newspapers with an eye to deserving organizations. Then, quarterly, they sat down together and divided the accumulated amount in their tithe account into four equal parts. In some categories, they donated the whole quarter to one organization; in other categories, they shared the accumulation among several organizations. They wrote short covering letters thanking the organization for the good work that they do, encouraging them to continue.

Larry and Belinda found that this practice gave them great joy. Everything about it, from depositing the 10 percent to mailing the checks and receiving thank you letters, made them feel wealthy. They were acting as if they were philanthropists. And guess what—they are philanthropists. Their 10 percent is out there doing good in the world as it is doing good for Larry and Belinda—helping them to feel wealthy and significantly increasing their sense of contribution and deservingness.

I have a client, Kathleen, who puts away one-half of her earnings to invest in her own spiritual growth. She uses this money for classes, workshops, seminars, books, tapes and spiritual trips. She is investing heavily in her own spiritual growth, which will radically improve the quality of her life and increase her finances.

I encourage you to consider tithing. Try it for a time. See if it doesn't immediately give you an experience of prosperity to give away money to worthwhile organizations that you would like to help succeed. By acting as if you were a philanthropist, you will certainly become one.

EXERCISES

Contemplate the following questions and write your answers in your journal or notebook:

1. What are your beliefs that keep you from having money? List at least five.
2. What are your fears about money? List at least five.
3. How do you feel about touching your bills? Your money?
4. How do you feel about spending money?
5. Do you use paper money or credit card or debit/ATM card?
6. If you use your credit card, really start to look at those purchases and see if those items or material things are something you genuinely need. The awareness will help you not to spend endlessly. Ask yourself:
   • Is it moving me forward?
   • Do I really need to take that trip?
   • Do I need those clothes?
7. Stay in the outflow. Give money to good causes, meaning charities and people who will really value your gift. Make a list of any charities you like and want to support with gifts.
8. Pick one charity every six months and contribute. Write a check or give them cash. Receive a receipt.
9. Do you attempt to control anyone or anything with money? If so, make a list of whom and why.
10. If you become the wealthy and prosperous person you would like to be, who would this threaten in your life? Who might walk away from you?
11. How do you feel about asking for a raise from your employer? Now activate your power of choice. You choose to have enough money always. Choose not to blame anyone or any condition on your financial situation.

🍂 AFFIRMATIONS 🍂

Write and speak the following affirmations:

1. I am a money magnet.
2. I enjoy money and I enjoy receiving money.
3. I enjoy spending money wisely.
4. I always have enough money to do exactly what I choose to do.
5. I love money and money loves me.
6. The more money I share with my family and friends, the more I receive.
7. I trust that my supply of money is always unlimited.
8. I forgive all my issues of money and only accept the best!
9. I have no credit card debt or debt with others.
10. I am a spiritual being and a wealthy, prosperous individual now!

9

Living in Service

We have had several opportunities to consider that in the Spiritual Zone we are no longer living in the delusion of separation. Through forgiveness and at-one-ment, we have reconnected our consciousness to the Universal source. In the Spiritual Zone we know that we are not separate beings; rather, we recognize ourselves as unique manifestations of the one Universal source. In this state of conscious connectedness, we experience a more highly attuned access to other manifestations of life. This shows up, as we have discussed, as increased intuition, deepened empathy and sympathy, and heartfelt, motivating compassion. In the Spiritual Zone, our hearts are newly opened to the experiences of our fellow human travelers; we are more highly attuned to feel their joy and their pain, their successes and their needs because we are awakened to that part of ourselves that overlaps with them. Many human beings who have accessed the Spiritual Zone will experience their spiritual fulfillment by choosing lives of service.

"Higher" Consciousness

In the higher consciousness of the Spiritual Zone we have access to the bigger pictures of life. The word "higher" truly works here: the higher we rise above the details of earth, the broader the panorama of life we can access. This image works literally as well as figuratively. There are moving stories from many of the astronauts, recounting their life-changing experiences that resulted from having observed the beauty and vulnerability of our "blue planet" from space.

Navy Captain Dr. Edgar Mitchell, of the Apollo 14 mission, was the sixth man to walk on the moon. On his return journey, hurling

111

earthwards through space, Dr. Mitchell was overcome by such a profound sense of Universal connectedness that he knew his life would never be the same. He intuitively sensed that he, his fellow astronauts and the earth itself all somehow shared the same consciousness. Upon returning to earth, Dr. Mitchell founded the Institute of Noetic Science (IONS), a global wisdom society in which consciousness, spirituality and love are at the center of life. The IONS purpose is just what you might expect from an organization founded by a man dedicated to spiritual service: "To explore consciousness for a world awakening—where together we discover and learn to develop our individual and collective potentials—through frontier science, personal inquiry, and learning communities."

Dr. Mitchell's awakening experience is perhaps more dramatically illustrated than most, but it is nonetheless only one of millions of stories of individuals who have entered into the Spiritual Zone. In the Zone, we are likely to reevaluate our lives and commitments. Many of us will, like Dr Mitchell, decide to direct our energies and pursuits toward deepening and broadening the Zone experience—so that it is more readily accessible to others and continually more meaningful to ourselves.

This is one of the miraculous aspects of life in the Zone. We experience a personal connection to all humankind, and we feel drawn by that connection to offer our skills and energies in service to others. As each of us feels a deep, personal, steadfast connection to our immediate loved ones, we now begin to resonate with all people in a similar way, as brothers and sisters in our human family. This doesn't mean we all have to leave our careers as astronauts and business people, but I believe it does mean that we will inevitably bring more of our Spiritual Zone capacities to those careers. Whatever we are doing with our lives, we will be doing it with more intention, more mindfulness and more compassion for the others with whom we interact.

This is because, as Zone denizens, we have awakened more and deeper capacities in ourselves. We may feel greater responsibilities that also come with our awakening, but I don't believe these are externally mandated; instead, we feel compelled at a soul level to be helpful to our brothers and sisters who need our help. The origin of our drive to be of service may be simplified as a conscious spirit of fraternity, but the manifestation of how we choose to serve can bring grand and complex changes—as demonstrated by Dr. Mitchell's experience of transitioning from Apollo astronaut to founder of a spiritual foundation. You have exciting life opportunities to look forward to now that you have chosen the Spiritual Zone.

Go Deep!

Going deeply into spiritual service has been my personal experience. I touched on my entry into the Spiritual Zone at the beginning of this book, but I want to synopsize it again here. I had always worked in a service capacity, first as a personal assistant to several Hollywood actors and celebrities, and then as an agent and personal manager. I made a trip to Paris, where I discovered a profoundly deep familiarity, as though I had lived a Parisian life before. Remarkable things started happening to me. In a Paris nightclub, I sang a song from *Grease* (in which I had performed in Los Angeles) and that led surprisingly to a sudden recording contract. With the contract in place, I felt that it was time for me to put down roots in Paris. I returned to LA, dissolved my business, and returned as quickly as I could to my anticipated new life in France.

As soon as I arrived, I called the record company—and was devastated to learn that my contract had been cancelled. My hope for success and security had vanished into thin air! I went into an emotional tailspin, desperate for guidance. I went to the Cathedral of Notre-Dame every day for three weeks and prayed for guidance about what I should do. On the third day of the third week I experienced a revelatory vision. Sitting alone in a pew in the unusually empty church, I was suddenly beckoned to look up. From the ceiling of the cathedral, a brilliant vortex of purple light flowed down on to me, and in a twinkling I saw seven angels dancing around me. They whirled around me and spoke to me telepathically. They reassured me that I was correct in coming to France, and encouraged me to trust. My guardian angel, the Archangel Michael, made himself known to me, speaking his name. He continued to reassure me that all was well. His angelic energy was amazing—warm, buoyant, strong, holding me in calm security.

I walked back to my apartment and the phone rang. It was a friend offering me a free place to stay. The rest of the trip continued to fall together like that in a series of miracles. I came to understand that I was in France to have this particular experience of meeting Archangel Michael, and that I was being prepared for my life's work: spreading healing, joy, fulfilment, exultation, purpose and love; and helping others to awaken to their lives in the Spiritual Zone.

So here I am, writing to you about service. I had spent most of my previous career in service to others, but now I am working in service to our spirituality. My relations with my private clients and seminar audiences are profound and deep and intuitive. Living deep in the Zone, I have access to profound levels of empathy and compassion, which both inspire me to help others, and also enable me to clearly intuit exactly how I can best lend help in any given circumstance.

As you develop your familiarity with the Spiritual Zone, you will become expert in identifying your end results, acting as if, and keeping on track to create the life you want. These are the practical skills of how to make your life work for you in the way that you want. The longer and more intentionally you reside in the Zone, the deeper you will penetrate it.

Meaningful Pursuits

It has been my experience that long-time Zone residents are called to become powerful forces for service. This is not a requirement, but it does seem to happen. Once you have created the love partnership that you want and the job that you want and the house and the car that you want—all the external things that you think you want—you will find yourself seeking deeper and more meaningful pursuits. You will believe in your capacity to achieve anything, and therefore you will want to end world hunger and establish world peace. You will become so finely tuned to the needs of others—individuals who share your personal life, people at large around the world, the earth itself—that you will feel the drive to devote your enlightened capacities to spiritual service.

Entering into and dwelling in the Spiritual Zone, you will soon come to understand that scarcity is an illusion. Scarcity—the basis for world economic systems, and a leading cause of strife, wars, suffering, hunger and death—*is an illusion*. It is an illusion that reigns outside the Zone, where popular understanding is that the more you have, the less I have. In spiritual reality this is simply not true. First, the source is unlimited; we can create unlimited anything. Second, there is no true separation between you and me—we are all a part of Universal Consciousness, just as Edgar Mitchell experienced while racing back to Earth after his walk on the moon. In reality, the more *you* have, the more *I* have—*because we are one*. In the Spiritual Zone we feel a visceral experience of this unity. We no longer approach life from the point of an isolated, separated self; instead, we identify with the whole of which we are a unique part.

Have you ever played with a hologram? If you take a hologram and cut or break it apart, you will discover that each smaller piece contains the entire image of the whole that it once composed. This is a handy visual aid that can help you to picture your part in the whole of life. As a deeply, consciously connected part of the whole of life, our sense of self is expanded to include all of life. Therefore, our self-interest arises out of this experience of one-ness: what is good for you innately serves my self-interest. Quite simply, the more I am able to serve you, the more fulfilled I become. I no longer identify with scarcity, so serving you doesn't cost me a thing—it only benefits me. It fills me up. Serving others becomes my selfish need. How's that for a radical thought?

I can cite countless examples of people who have awakened to their highest destinies living in the Spiritual Zone. Earlier in this book, we talked about Mother Teresa and Gandhi and St. Francis. These are individuals we commonly and formally refer to as saints—yet they were only acting in their spiritual self-interest. They were individuals with highly developed consciousness who spent their lives in pursuit of personal fulfillment—which was serving the One Spirit. Popular culture, which is what for the most part exists outside the Zone, saw Mother Teresa as an unusually self-sacrificing kind of superwoman. From that narrow, scarce, delusional perspective, we were encouraged to see her as a living miracle for her willingness to subordinate her personal comforts to helping Calcutta's sick and poor. Yet in her awakened Zone state, what could give Mother Teresa more satisfaction than alleviating the suffering of her sisters and brothers? Her saintliness arises out of her clarity about the oneness of all life.

Do you remember my client, Sarah, the kindergarten teacher I introduced you to in Chapter Three? Sarah is an everyday example of someone who, after entering into the Spiritual Zone, has given her life over to service. She felt called to work with young children. Except for her considerable experiences as a mother of two, she hadn't really trained for a teaching career. Yet, she felt called. Sarah had done a great deal of spiritual work—study, yoga, meditation. She had awakened her consciousness and was deeply aware that her life was a series of choices to be made mindfully. Before she took time off to raise her young children, Sarah had worked as a pastry chef at a high-end San Francisco restaurant; she was very highly regarded in the food industry and had even been approached to do a dessert cookbook. When she was pregnant with her first child, she stopped working and figured she would return to her profession one day. She continued to think this throughout her second pregnancy and the several years when her children were young.

One morning, when her younger child was in first grade, Sarah woke up feeling an urgency to work with young children. She describes it as a deep knowing, as if it had always been there inside her, but she had failed to notice it until that day. This was in the spring. Sarah visited a preschool in her neighborhood. She didn't know much about it, but had heard good things from her friends with kids. She just followed an impulse to stop by on her way home from the grocery. She met the director as she approached the building, and said honestly—surprising herself—that she had awakened that morning feeling that she was to begin working with young children. She apologized for being spontaneous, but asked if she could see the school and perhaps apply for an assistant position for the coming September. The director looked a little astonished; she told Sarah that an assistant had just given notice that morning. She asked whether Sarah would be interested in starting work the following Monday.

This is what happens when you align with your truth. The Universe has been waiting for you to open the door. Sarah did start working the next Monday, and by the following September she was the lead kindergarten teacher in another school. She explained to me that she felt compelled to work with young children, who are still new to physical incarnation. She felt that she could understand their confusion in coming to terms with physical reality and that she could reassure them by meeting them as spiritual beings and ensuring that they were seen and honored and understood. Sarah believes that she was spiritually called by the children who are now students in her class. She feels that she made a spiritual agreement with them that she would be here to greet them, reassure them and teach them as they stepped out of the cozy womb of their families and into the outside world as five-year-old kindergarteners.

Sarah starts her day early each morning, meditating on her children before going to school, and then works late hours at home after her own children are in bed, preparing for the next day. She ends her day meditating on each child before going to sleep. Sarah works terrifically long hours, but she does not feel that she is making a sacrifice; she feels filled up by her service because she honors her class of children as high spiritual beings who have come to Earth to make a difference. She feels thrilled to have an opportunity to meet these young children in the Spiritual Zone, to reassure them simply by her loving presence that the Zone does exist in the incarnate adult world and that they can trust that it is real. Sarah feels honored to be of service to these children; she hopes that her presence in their young lives will assure them that they can safely bring their biggest spiritual selves here to physical reality.

Through her awakened spiritual intention in working with children, Sarah is enabling them to retain the spiritual consciousness that they brought to this incarnation. All our souls were high when we first came into this world, but we have been injured and reduced and whittled upon by an unconscious adult society. Because of Sarah's guidance, her kindergarteners will not have to stray so far from spiritual reality as so many of us have done, only to find our way back now in our thirties and forties and fifties and sixties. Imagine the impact on the world when all kindergarten children are met as spiritual beings and able to retain their spiritual consciousness. Imagine a whole generation of young people who have grown up fully conscious of their spiritual paths, a generation who don't have to suffer the "stranger in a strange land" phenomenon of growing up in a delusional, materialistic world. These children—Sarah's kindergarteners—are tomorrow's leaders. They will grow up recognizing their calling as servers of Universal spirit. This is the grand future of our children and grandchildren. This is the vision that Sarah has been called to bring forth. No wonder her life of service brings her such great joy.

Joy is an exhilarating expression of who we are as creative spiritual beings. It is a force that will magnetize your desires to you. It is inherently attractive, bringing community support. Sarah's kindergarten children are little joy beings whose desires will be readily met because their energy is so attractive. Their powers of manifestation are invincible. Protected by Sarah, their server, they expect with all their hearts that the world will love them.

Loving Ourselves as a Service to Others

Babies arrive in physical reality ready to love themselves. It is their negative experiences of a hostile, materialistic world that disenfranchise them from their innate power of self-love. This has tremendous trickle-down effects. I believe we cannot love one another more than we love ourselves. How much we love ourselves sets the level for our capacity to love others. Love, like service, is not a self-sacrificing act. There is no scarcity of love in the world. Love is an infinite commodity. The more love we give the more love we have. The more love we have the more love we attract. Imagine the love that comes back to Sarah from her twenty soulfully appreciative children. Imagine the love that was bestowed upon Mother Teresa by the poor of Calcutta or St. Francis by the poor of Assisi or Gandhi by the masses in India. Love was their reward for their lives of service.

Consider some of the leaders of the world who have committed themselves to selfless service. I can promise you that Nobel Peace Prize winners Jimmy Carter, Nelson Mandela, Mother Teresa and the Dalai Lama love themselves. As did Martin Luther King, Jr. None of these people devoted their lives to service as a penance because they had a guilty conscience. None of them devoted their lives to service because they wanted fame or ego gratification. Each of them was called to service by their higher consciousness. By choosing a spiritual path of serving others, they live in an atmosphere of love and gratitude. The more they love themselves the more love they have to share with others through their service. The more service they offer, the more they feel they are meeting their life purpose.

I invite you to open yourself to the possibility that, in the Spiritual Zone, you, too, will find yourself called to fulfillment through a life of service. This is not to say that you need to relinquish your current career or interests—you may in fact deepen longstanding commitments by bringing a new attitude of spiritual service to these endeavors. By establishing a personal habit of asking how you can bring loving service to every situation you encounter, you will be sharing the high spiritual energy of the Zone with everyone you come in contact with. Then feel your capacities deepen and expand. Then feel your fulfillment and self-worth blossom. Then feel the love pour into your life.

EXERCISES

Contemplate the following questions and write your answers in your journal or notebook:

STEP ONE
1. If you knew you could make no mistakes, what would you really do with your life?
2. If you never had to worry about finances and money ever again, what would you do?
3. If you knew no one would ever judge you in life, what would you do?
4. Do you feel you have failed in this life?
5. What would you really love to do?

STEP TWO
1. How do you perceive life and yourself?
2. How do other people perceive you?

3. My life right now is _____.
4. My financial situation is _____.
5. The most important thing in my life is _____.
6. On a 1 to 10 scale, how would you rate yourself?
7. Because?

By writing all these items I want you to start to change your belief system. The ego will try to take over, and fear may enter into your thinking. The action steps are to look at your answers closely.

Redo the questions again—with end-result answers this time—answers that are coming from the place of love and truth.

STEP THREE

Complete the following:

1. I perceive myself as others perceive me as
2. My life is
3. My finances are
4. The most important thing in my life is
5. I rate myself a

Congratulations! You have aligned your soul's purpose with your true self.

🌰 AFFIRMATIONS 🌰

Write and speak the following affirmations:

1. It's okay for me to give love and acceptance to others.
2. I am worthy and deserving.
3. I release myself from the bondage of resentment and free myself from all others who do not support my vision.
4. I do not control others by guilt.
5. I am accepting myself for being exactly where I need to be in my life.
6. I am lovingly appreciating myself and all others.
7. I have no guilt or shame in my life.
8. I am trusting the Universe to provide complete clarity in my life. Now!

10

Visualizing the Life
That You Want

Visualization is the most effective tool for manifesting in the Spiritual Zone. What you picture, you can create.

Of the five physical senses, our visual acuity is our most highly developed and most frequently relied upon. We think in pictures. We "picture" our Italian vacation spots: the elegant, flowered curves of the Spanish steps, the spectacular extravagance of the Trevi Fountain, the medallion of blue sky shining through the roof of the Pantheon. We visualize in infinite colors and the finest detail. We use the expression "I see" to indicate that we understand something. Of the many learning styles, the visual learner is the most common. They need to see a diagram, an illustration on the blackboard, a map when figuring directions. They think in pictures. They store memory in pictures. They create their future in pictures.

Visualizing is our most effective tool for getting us to our end results. The more time we spend imagining a scene or a picture, the more clarity we bring to the detail. The more specific details that we picture, the more we are able to ground our visualization in physical reality. Visualization helps us to establish all the details of the "what" that we want, feeding the Universe more specific directions as it proceeds to take care of the "how."

A Picture Story

Contemplate the following exercise to experience the power of effective visualization: picture yourself walking down an empty, narrow country road. There are no cars. Far off in the distance, sitting on a small rise to the left, is a structure. As you progress down the road, you recognize that in fact you are looking at two structures; a little further and you realize one of them, the one closest to you, is a house. Behind it is a barn, once painted red, now faded to a weathered brick color. The house is a single story, unpainted wooden structure with a long covered porch that wraps around the corner and out of sight. A few wide steps lead up to the porch. Something is moving rhythmically on the porch—a swing? A rocking chair? A small trail of dust travels down the driveway towards the main road. You look hard to see what is making the dust. You don't see a car. Is it a pedestrian? A bicycle? In several more paces you see that it might be a horse; no, it is a dog, a very large brown dog. A Great Dane? No, a hound of some kind. As you hear his faint bark, you see one of the window shades rise. A figure in the window looks out, first at the dog, then at you, a long distance up the road. A tired, split-rail fence rambles along the road, barely containing an unruly field of browning cornstalks.

The front door is painted periwinkle. It looks freshly painted, its brilliant presence a celebration against the still monochrome of the weathered cedar siding, the dun fields, the dirt driveway, the brown dog, the dust. Someone has made a happy periwinkle statement. It is a swing on the porch, moving gently forward and back. Is someone swinging in it? Yes, lying down. A little closer and you determine it's a young girl. She's lying on the seat in a plain dress, one barefooted leg hanging over, the toes occasionally offering a gentle push against the floorboards. Her hair is in an unruly braid, straw-blonde. A piebald cat is stretched out on the porch railing. There's an old red tricycle with a white fender and a thin pile of newspapers next to the seat. A pale green drinking glass is on the floor. The one who raised the shade inside had been reading the paper on the porch earlier, you figure. Drinking an iced tea.

You're at the driveway now, walking up the shallow slope. The dog has approached you, no longer barking. His long tail wags. You let him sniff your hand, then you scratch behind his ears. Now you're friends. He wears no collar. His ears are silken and floppy, unusually floppy for a hound. He's big. A Rhodesian ridgeback, maybe, but ridgeless. Dead sunflowers line the driveway, hanging their heavy, seeded heads in shame over lost beauty. The dog walks at your side. You feel welcomed. To your right, a tire swing hangs in a live oak. The girl on the porch swing sits up. You wave to her and she takes her thumb from her mouth and tentatively raises her hand to you with a closed-mouth smile.

A flagstone path leads through neglected grass to the porch steps. A flowerpot of orange marigolds sits on the right side of the middle step; beside it is an empty cereal bowl with a spoon in it. The child walks toward you. She is small, maybe five years old. She has blue eyes and a few freckles on her cheeks. Her dress is pale yellow, gathered at the waist. There is a scab on her left knee and a line faintly imprinted on her right cheek from where she was lying against the board of the swing. Needing to hold something, she picks up the cat. It lies complacently in the crook of her arm. You notice a dimple in her elbow. The cat jumps from her arms and down the steps, rubs against your khakis at your left ankle. The child reaches out to you in a welcoming hug.

I use this picture story as an example of how a visualized scene can become increasingly real as you fill in the details. From a vague, distant farmhouse on a hill, our visualization took on specific, unique life through the added details as we got closer: the dead sunflowers, the periwinkle door, the scab on the girl's knee. This is the key to success in using visualization as an effective tool in creating our end results. The more exact and detailed we are in picturing what it is we want, the more readily the Universal energy can breathe life into all the specifics of our imaginings.

Your Life as a Blank Canvas

Consider that you are a child who knows no limits. Imagine that I gave you some art supplies—oil paints, fine brushes and a primed canvas—and I asked you to paint a picture of your ideal life, whatever you want it to be. You may paint absolutely anything. It is just for you. No one will judge it. What do you see in this painting?

Each moment of your life, you have this canvas before you and you are free to do with it as you choose. This is always your choice. In your paintbrush you hold the power to create the life you want. The finer the details you are able to establish, the more exactly you identify the specifics of your life. The more specific, the easier it is for Universal energy to breathe into your picture and deliver it to you in three-dimensional physical reality.

While I use painting as a metaphor, your life itself is indeed a work of art. It is perfectly unique and solely yours. Only you are able to visualize your life. Only you are capable of creating it. This is both an incredible gift and an enormous responsibility. Will you give yourself permission to create for yourself what you truly want?

Consciously or unconsciously, you are creating for yourself all the time. Is the life you have the life you want to be creating for yourself? If so, you have cause to celebrate! If you are not pleased by your life, it is time to visualize something different. You have the canvas and the brushes. What do you want to invite into your life? Whom do you want to invite? What do you want to create? Your choices are endless, and you are always inspired. Quiet yourself and listen for your desires in the quiet of your own heart. Identify them and visualize them in all their detailed particulars.

Think of the visualization of the young girl on the farmhouse porch. Make your own picture of your desires for your life. Starting out it will be general. That's okay. A painter begins with simple shapes. The secret is never to stop identifying the details. Your visualization task is to fine-tune the details until you become very familiar with the most intimate particulars of what it is that you want for yourself. Then you know exactly where you are headed in life and you can identify the step-by-step directions that will take you there. If your visualization isn't perfectly clear, you will be unsure how to get to it and you'll get stalled and sidetracked along the way.

The Masterpiece of You

Find a quiet place. Visualize a space in your heart that holds what you deserve to create for yourself in this lifetime. Breathe into that space, letting go of all judgments. Take your time. After you have found that comfort zone and rested there for a while, notice what it is you want to create for your life at this particular moment. Thank your heart for its active presence in moving you into your creative space.

Now, picture yourself in your ideal art studio. Maybe it is a light-filled converted shed in your garden. It is sunny and comfortably warm. A small fountain on the patio outside bubbles soothingly in the background. Sunlight pools on the terracotta floor tiles. This is your ideal creative workspace. All your favorite art supplies are arranged on the butcher-block table before you. You have every creative tool imaginable. Notice canvas, brushes, the finest paints and oils, wood, metal, papers, water, rocks, fabrics and so much more. Notice all the other elements and tools. As you stand here in this ideal art studio, breathe into the artist in you, the creator. Take a long, slow, deep breath now.

As you create the work of art that represents what you have found in your heart, know that it is perfect. As you create your work of art, breathe your life into it. When it is complete, step back and take in its beauty and perfection. While you are embracing its beauty and perfection, remember that you can return to your art studio at any time and create again and again. Remember that you can create anything anew. Visualize an object from your studio that you can carry with you wherever you go, an object that will serve to remind you of the artistic and creative energy you hold to create for yourself in this life. You can visualize this reminder being with you at all times.

You Are Never Alone

Know that you are never alone, that with any heartfelt intention you set for yourself, you are guided beyond what you ever imagined. When you embrace your creativity, the Universe will show you the way. You will be brought into contact with whatever you need to manifest your visualized intention. Stay open to how help will show up in your life. It may not always be apparent at first glance. It's there. Trust it. Allow the magic to unfold. Open yourself to the serendipity, to the miracles. They're happening all around you and for you.

EXERCISES

I want you to do a visualization checklist with me. Return to this list, or any individual items on it, as often as you like to reinforce specific areas.

1. In this exercise I don't want you to write. I want you to feel, trust and be. Think of yourself as a blank canvas. I have just given you a box of beautiful, high-quality, colorful paints. In your mind, paint me a picture of yourself.
2. Close your eyes and think about:
   • How do you want your life to be?
   • What do you want it to look like?
   • How do you want to look?
3. Really believe that this is all possible. You can have all of this. Now write: I accept this in my life now!
4. Write: I am grateful for all these blessings and for the knowledge that my higher self is receiving.
5. Think of a time that was the best time in your life. Now close your eyes and visualize that place, the feelings, people and events—right now.
6. Remember the feeling of that joy and happiness it brought you. Now bring that feeling into your current everyday life.
7. Before you take any actions or decisions in your life, ask yourself:
   • What will the result be?
   • Is it worth it?
   • Do I really want that?
8. Start to rely on your inner voice. Trusting yourself is an important part of this work.
9. Start to operate from a world of love and compassion. Before you do anything, ask yourself: is this action coming from my ego mind? Or from my loving, compassionate self? Wait for the answer—it will be given to you. Listen and accept it.

🍂 AFFIRMATIONS 🍂

Write and speak the following affirmations, returning to reinforce ones that have particular resonance for you:

1. Today is the first day of the rest of my life!
2. I am grateful, compassionate and appreciative for everyone and everything in my life.
3. I allow my true love into my life.
4. I am experiencing only feelings of love, kindness and compassion.
5. I complete all my projects and ideas, and I am compensated with unlimited finances.
6. All my dreams are fulfilled.
7. I have no limitations in my consciousness.
8. I have stamina and persistence in my life.
9. All my affirmations become truth for me in my life, now!

Afterword

Having read the chapters and worked through the exercises and affirmations of this book, you have learned how to get to the Spiritual Zone by waking up your awareness, letting go of your emotional past and practicing forgiveness to have the love you deserve. You have learned how to stay in the Spiritual Zone by activating your power of choice, recognizing you have support and changing old patterns. And now, you have learned how to manifest in the Spiritual Zone by getting to know yourself as a creator, practicing visualization, financial freedom and service to others. If you have been mindful and diligent along the way, by now you will have begun to have an authentic and comprehensive personal experience of life in the Spiritual Zone.

You will have identified a specific traveling companion and perhaps several or even many spiritual allies along the way. As you practice mindful presence in the Zone you will encounter more and more spiritual allies as you go about your daily life. Know always that I am your fellow traveler, that you are never alone on this path. If you doubt or slip, reread this book—my energy and presence are stored here for you in these directions and words of encouragement.

I wish for you to know the heart-brimming joy that you will feel as you experience the flow of your own spirituality. Your loving energy and confidence in spiritual abundance attracts love and all kinds of abundant resources into your life. Remembering that we are all one—I grow and flourish with you as your commitment to the Spiritual Zone propels you further into love and light.

Enjoy the journey!
Love,
Gary

Postscript

Postcards from the Spiritual Zone

Since lecturing and leading seminars about the Spiritual Zone, I frequently hear from participants about the joys, successes and miracles that have come into their lives since consciously entering the Zone. I have chosen to share some of these "postcards" from your fellow travelers with the hope that you find comfort and inspiration in them. In consideration of the senders, I have identified them by first names only.

FROM DONNA:

I attended a Spiritual Zone workshop, and had the pleasure of being chosen as Gary's second participant. I was rather amazed at how difficult it was for me to say, "I am just as good as all of you," and truly believe it. But something happened while standing there with a microphone in my hand, in front of an entire audience. Perhaps it was my guardian angel whispering in my ear, "Say it, because it is true, and because your photography career means more to you than anything else in the world." Thanks to Spiritual Zone guidance, I was able to express this affirmation. When I arrived home after the seminar, a letter was waiting for me from the International Library of Photography. My photo contest entry had been advanced to semi-finalist, and since then my photograph has been chosen to be published in a forthcoming anthology.

FROM BRIAN:

After attending a Spiritual Zone workshop, I began to manifest my positive energy and throw it out there into the Universe. Within two weeks, many exciting opportunities in my acting career started to fall into place. The phone was ringing off the hook! I was getting booked for auditions and work. I landed two lucrative national commercials in that two-week period after the workshop. I can feel the Spiritual Zone working deep inside me and also around me externally. I know from my experience that Gary is "right on" with this information.

FROM AMANDA:

While reading *May the Angels Be with You,* I said out loud, "I'd love to meet Gary Quinn, go to one of his workshops and have a private consultation." Three months later, I discovered that Gary would be leading a workshop in Toronto at the same time I was planning to visit—a "miracle" in its own right. I immediately enrolled in the workshop and I've been continuing to manifest miraculously in the Spiritual Zone ever since.

FROM MARY-JO:

While working for years as a lawyer, I always wanted to be an artist. When I attended Gary's talk about the Spiritual Zone, I left so inspired that I kept telling myself I was an artist. I worked with the affirmation that "I am that world-renowned artist"—and the last two months have been incredible. I just finished my first art show in which I sold all my work, and I also got my first commissions. I can only hope that other people can take that first step toward living in the Spiritual Zone. It is an incredible feeling to love what I do and be appreciated and compensated for it.

FROM SHARON:

I have been intentionally living in the Spiritual Zone for about two years. A year ago, feeling quite priced out of the local real estate market, I used Zone principles and focused my end result on a house that I could afford to buy. I gave myself a four-month deadline and visualized an affordable old house that could be renovated. I responded to an ad for the possibility of buying a 1904 historic home—for $1 from the city of Portland. The catch was that you had to move the house off their property. They would contribute $20,000 to the moving costs. We are now unpacking and signing the final papers for this lovely old family home. Manifesting in the Spiritual Zone really works!

From Leslie:

Gary Quinn has taught both my daughter and me how to live in the Spiritual Zone. We were "to act-as-if" my daughter already has a successful modeling career—and she would indeed become successful. We have focused on this end result and her career is now on a very positive track! She is appearing in many magazines, on billboards, the *Today Show* and in music videos. The Spiritual Zone principles truly bring miracles into manifestation.

From Tammy:

I was ill and faced many differing opinions about how to treat hypoglycemia, hypothyroidism and panic attacks. It seemed that I would try something and feel worse instead of better. After attending a Spiritual Zone workshop I truly committed to my healing journey. I can finally say that I feel secure in my healing, and believe that good things are happening in my life. Each day, I feel stronger and more loving and alive than I have in the past ten years.

From David:

Intentionally living in the Spiritual Zone has created a shift in my consciousness from stress to relaxation and end results. I have created a successful new business and have met my new wife. I just purchased our "dream house" in Hawaii. Consciously loving myself and focusing attention on my end results have brought me the life I've always dreamed of. Try living in the Spiritual Zone. I guarantee you'll love it!

Conscientious Zone Reading

Akers, Keith, *A Vegetarian Sourcebook,* Vegetarian Press, Arlington, Va., 1983

Braden, Gregg, *Walking Between the Worlds: The Science of Compassion,* Radio Bookstore Press, Washington, 1997

Chopra, Deepak, *The Seven Spiritual Laws of Success,* Amber-Allen, San Rafael, 1994

Cole-Whittaker, Terry, *Every Saint Has a Past, Every Sinner a Future,* Jeremy P. Tarcher/Puttnam, New York, 2001

Dayton, Tian, *The Magic of Forgiveness,* Health Communications, Deerfield Beach, 2003

Dwoskin, Hale, *The Sedona Method,* Sedona Press, Sedona, 2003

Finley, Guy, *Freedom from the Ties That Bind,* Llewellyn Publications, St. Paul, 2000

Ford, Debbie, *The Secret of the Shadow,* Hodder Mobius, London, 2002

Ford, Debbie, *The Right Questions,* Hodder Mobius, London, 2004

Gooch, Brad, *Godtalk,* Alfred A. Knopf, New York, 2002

Hamilton, Maggie, *Coming Home,* Viking Press/Penguin Group, London, 2002

Hemingway, Mariel, *Finding My Balance,* Simon & Schuster, New York, 2003

Henner, Marilu, *Total Health Makeover,* HarperCollins, London, 1998

Humphrey, Naomi, *Understanding Meditation,* HarperCollins, London, 1998

Inglis, Les, *Diet for a Gentle World,* Avery Press, London, 2000

Myss, Carolyn, *Sacred Contracts,* Three Rivers Press, New York, 2003

Okawa, Ryuo, *The Starting Point of Happiness,* Lantern Books, New York, 2001

Ruiz, Don Miguel, *The Four Agreements,* Amber-Allen, San Rafael, 1997

Sasson, Gahl and Weinstein, Steve, *A Wish Can Change Your Life,* Fireside/Simon & Schuster, New York, 2003

Steinman, David, *Diet for a Poisoned Planet,* Harmony Books, New York, 1990

Titmuss, Christopher, *Mindfulness for Everyday Living,* Godsfield Press, London, 2002

Yogananda Paramahansa, *Man's Eternal Quest,* Self Realization Fellowship, Los Angeles, 1982

Yogananda Paramahansa, *To Be Victorious in Life,* Self Realization Center, Los Angeles, 2002

Acknowledgments

I acknowledge the immeasurable contribution of all the people who have supported me as a person and as an intuitive-motivational-life coach. Especially the many friends, clients and special people I have had the privilege to work with—because ultimately, everyone in our lives supports our spiritual enlightenment and growth.

First and foremost, this book could not have been written without the professional help of Chip Romer. Your input has been so appreciated and thank you for your brilliant skills.

Barbara Moulton, my agent and guiding light. Thank you for your trust, vision, friendship and patience. I am grateful for your continuous commitment to my work.

Patricia Gift, thank you for your devotion, support and love. You have always inspired me to achieve only the best.

Special thanks to all at Hodder & Stoughton: Rowena Webb, Isabel Duffy, Briar Silich, Helen Coyle, Eleni and Jacqui Lewis for allowing my work to impact the world. Your vision made this book possible. Thank you.

Thank you: HCI/Health Communications Inc., Amy Hughes, Peter Vegso and Gary Seidler for your vision and persistence. Thank you, Bret Witter, Tom Sand and Kim Weiss.

Debbie Luican, Nancy Burke, Elizabeth and Christopher Day, Ira Streitfeld, Deb Ingersol and Chad Edwards. Thank you for your insight and your vision to heal this earth together.

Thank you, Robert Lee/Bayonne Entertainment, for bringing my work to television.

Thank you, REP—Rebel Entertainment Partners, Inc., Talent Agency. Thank you, Richard Lawrence, Susan Haber, Laura Hartman, Angie White, Dawn and Nick—for bringing my work to television.

Thank you, Evelyn M. Dalton and Patricia Q., for your constant support and love. You are both truly amazing!

Thank you, Christopher Watt, for your love, support and enthusiasm.

Thank you, Harold Dupré, for your artistic talents, support and friendship.

Thank you, Ute Ville, Jane Damian and Nastassja Kinski, for your friendship and love.

Thank you, John Maroney, Tom Janczur and Damon Miller, for your constant friendship.

Thank you, Velma Cato, for your talent, friendship, belief and vision.

Thank you, Bruce R. Hatton, CPA, for your constant help and support.

Thank you, Dave Harding, for your insight and support.

Thank you, Christin Tippets, Sun Valley, Idaho Chamber of Commerce, Sherry Daech, Carol Waller, Connie Kemmerer, Midge Woods, Marcia Duff and Ann Down, for your energy and support.

Thank you, Amy Harris and Tracy, for your hard work, friendship and love.

Thank you, Cheryl Welch, for your love, insight, intention and Chapter One Bookstore.

Thank you, Sante Losio and Doriana Mazola, for your friendship.

Thank you, Nik Sakellarides, for your spiritual musical talents.

Thank you, Glennyce S. Eckersley, for your partnership, love and talents!

Thank you, Amelia Kinkade, for your friendship, support and insight!

Thank you, Mason Citarello and staff at Mason Jar.

Thank you, Deborah Molinari, for your talents and spirit.

Thank you, Peppe Miele for Napoletana! Italia! Marina Del Rey!

Thank you, Andreas Kurz and Iris Loesel, for your love and friendship.

Thank you, Anne Taylor, for your constant loving insight and illumination.

Thank you, Jo Carey and The Bodhi Tree Bookstore, for your support.

Thank you, Elena Sahagun, for our "PISCES" connection, friendship and love.

Thank you, Random House UK—Judith Kendra, Sarah Bennie and David Parrish.

Thank you, Random House Canada—Cathy Paine.

Thank you, Cheryl Murphy, for your hard work, partnership, friendship and your making a difference in children's lives.

Thank you, Nance Mitchell, for your life friendship and support of my work.

Thank you, Our Living Center staff and volunteers. My administrative assistant, Doriana Mazola. Thank you for giving so much of yourself.

Thank you, Kelly Wald, for your hard work and magical website designs.

Thank you, Shirley MacLaine and Brit Elder, for supporting my work and letting me change lives through the medium of your IE Radio show.

Special thanks to Linda Mize Kelley, Sr. Vice President at Lynk Sytems, Inc. It is a pleasure to share my life coaching principles to such an insightful Senior Vice President, and your incredible company. Thank you.

Thank you, Patricia J. Gannon Fleming, for your spiritual talents.

Thank you, Donna Dysonna of *Dysonna Magazine*.

Thank you, Nancy Bishop—*Venice Magazine*.

Thank you, Daniel Toll, Glen Hartford and Cinamour Entertainment.

Thank you, Linda Judy-Brim, Konrad Hoenig, Aquarius Calendars and Linda Truedeau.

Thank you, Leeza Gibbons, for your incredible spirit and support.

Thank you, Laa Joshua and Nina Paoulucci and Belinda DiBene, for your friendship.

Thank you, Dyan Cannon and Matlin Mirman, for your true friendship.

Thank you, Victoria Manjikian and Beaumont Products, Inc.

Thank you, Esther Williams, for your beauty, grace and your positive spiritual beliefs. I cherish our special times together and look forward to many more.

Thank you, Roberto Benigni, Geoffrey Rush, Vincent Schiavelli, Michael J. Pollard, Janet Caroll, John Travolta, Jonelle Allen, Rebekah Paltrow and Seal, for all your talents and the opportunity to connect with all of you!

Special thanks to the following people:

Paul Jackson, Mark Armstrong, Marina Schmidt, Mark Read, David Pond, Anoja Dias, Gina Webb, Sarah and R.Q., Kris Ayers, Ricky Strauss, Jacky Olitsky, Nancy Procter, Carol Dib, Zee Boyadjian, Donna Delory, Jerry Apadaca and Rochelle Vallese, Bron Annette Frehling, Sandra Mesa, Shannon Factor, Gail Pierson, Hilda, Delaina Mitchell, Rolanda Watts, Liza Sullivan, Sylvia Castillo, Dottie Galliano, Barbara Deutsch, Ken Campbell, Gloria Tredent, Francesca Moroder, Sharon Tay, Richard Ayoub, Lucia Moro, Brian Wright, Sally Lear, Mapi M., Shiela Huber, Toni Galardi, Michelle Franguel, Jean Louis and Peggy Dupre, Realtime, Kathy Talbot, SPANI, Marcelle Dupre, Lory Barra, Debbie Dalrymple—Hedra News, Gena Lee Nolin, Tara Rivas, Brad Gooch, Christine Thomas, Debbie Ford, Dana Ware, Ivan Allen, Ann Rutter, Rachel Miller, Monica Pelayo, Maggie Hamilton, Stephanie Scheier, Amanda Hayward, CFRB-Canada, Kavita Daswani, Karman Graham, Nididi Nkagbu, Rob Lloyd, Arielle Ford, Simone Vollmer, Diana Jordan, Doreen Virtue, Marcia Brandwynne, David Sersta, Marie Anne Guinto, Kim McArthur, Elisabeth Golden, Angela Quaranta, Helen Hoehne, Stephani Saible, Verna Hebling, Dr. Gerald Jampolsky, Keith Baker, Devin, Ashlee, Michael Franchino, Kate Bolyn, ANI, Michelle Collins, Concetta Tomei, Lacine Forbes, Leah Tenderfoot, Anna Gabriel Ouroumian, Maureen Driscoll, James Twyman, Elizabeth Stephens, Cheryl Eckler, Annie Zalezsak, Angela Quaranta, Christal Curry, David Jeans, Martin Allaire, Miriam Khullar, Kevin at World Travel, Glennyce Eckersley, Liz Guevara, Joann Hammond, Deepak Chopra, Denise Linn, Diana Kane Britt, Jana Halvorson, Nick Wilder, Mariel Hemingway, Bruno Allaire, Marc Henri Caillard, Eva Marie, Kurt Knutsson, Storm Balchunas, Kathryn Melton, Paulo Figueiredo, Sandra Cooper, The Learning Light, Kathy DeSantis, Louise Hay, The Voice Box—Traci Patton, Brent Backhus, Claudio and Adria Blotta, Terry Cole-Wittaker, Alternatives-UK—Richard Dunkerley and Steve Nobel, Victoria Stewart Glick, Deb Agam, Frank Smith, Caroline Sutherland, Craig Campabaso, Joy Todd, Herb & Lynda Tannen, Bridget Gibson, Cheray Unman, Lee Dos Santos, Carolyn Burdet, Jennifer and Courtney Eads, Peter & Karen Rafelson, Wilke Durand, Patricia Gaza de

Sullivan, Leslie Williams, Russ Pisano, Serafina Pechan, Kona Carmack, Don Skeoch, Gloria and Yvonne Ohayon, Maha Dib, Michel El Daher, Alexander Daou, Andrea Zanelli, Carol, Shannon and Brian Sheehan, Marie Rose Zard, Matthew Miley, Carol Campbell, Joan H. DeMayo, Frank Fischer, Angel and Eric R. Rhoades, Asha Madhawan, Douglas and Lisa Preston, Tracie Austin-Peters, Luc Leestemaker, Mary Griffin, Wally Barela, *Awareness Magazine*—Darby Davis, Rick, Irene Crandell, Barbara Groth, Sierra Dickens, Sadie Jacobs, Athenia, Jamie Kabler, Patrica Sardella, Mark Bass, Lillian Too, Joann Turner, Tim Burke, Shari Meyers Gantman, Laura Powers, Nicole Bilderback, Marc Malvin, Tom Butler, Kim Corbin, Wilke Durand, Sharon Botchway, Angella Conrad, Charlie Schlafke, Brent Backhus, Eric Tiperman and Craig, Marion Renk-Richardson, Harold A. Lancer, Brigette Schwenner, Mark Thallander, Joie Gaty, Stuart Benjamin, Mary Watt, Kim and Johan Uyttewaal, Jacqueline and Jerry Anderson, Maggie Roepke, Kevin Spirtis, Artie Cabrera, Andrea Morgan, Desomond and Beverly Hayes, Jennifer and Courtney Eads, Peter Kennedy, Wendy Peckingpaugh, Nadine Cutright, Sari Colt, Amanda Pisani, Shari Carr, Mutsumi and Paul Appleby, Mark and Amanda Hughes, Dr. David Walker, Janice O'Gara, Stephen Halpern, Gahl Sasson, Victoria Jennings, Hatty Hoover, Lucrietia Jones, Sasson, Eric and Karlyn Pipes-Nielson, Sandra Ingerman, Rebecca Lopez, Janet Wilder, Beverly, Johannterhoff Seminar House, Germany, Wolfgang and Uschi Maiworm, Ivan Kavalsky and Veronica De Laurentiis.

I THANK ALL OF YOU.

For anyone I have inadvertently missed, I hope you can forgive.

Our Living Center-Touchstone for Life Coaching Center

Contact Information for
Workshops, Classes and Training

Gary Quinn is the founder of Our Living Center-Touchstone for Life Coaching Center in Los Angeles, which trains and transforms individuals to create successful results in their lives. Gary Quinn and the staff of Our Living Center can help you to change your life, offering workshops, classes, private coaching, newsletters, weekend intensives, keynote speaking, consulting and training to become a certified Touchstone for Life Coach.

Our extensive and in-depth coaching training will give you the skills and confidence to become a Touchstone for Life Coach who can work to support individuals living in the Spiritual Zone. The Certified Touchstone for Life Coaching Program (CTLC) is a four-month intensive process that will guide you to discover and deliver your unique style while training you to become a Touchstone for Life Coach, using the tools and principles presented in *Living in the Spiritual Zone*.

For more information, contact or visit:

Our Living Center-Touchstone for Life
PO Box 16041
Beverly Hills, CA 90209 USA
www.ourlivingcenter.co
www.garyquinn.tv